DINNER for TWO

JULIE WAMPLER

DINNER for TWO

EASY AND INNOVATIVE RECIPES
FOR ONE, TWO, OR A FEW

JULIE WAMPLER

The Countryman Press
A division of W. W. Norton & Company
Independent Publishers Since 1923

The Countryman Press
www.countrymanpress.com

A division of W. W. Norton & Company, Inc.
500 Fifth Avenue, New York, NY 10110
www.wwnorton.com

For information about special discounts for bulk purchases, please contact
W. W. Norton Special Sales at specialsales@wwnorton.com or 800-233-4830.

Book design by Endpaper Studio
Printed in China

Dinner for Two
978-1-58157-289-6

10 9 8 7 6 5 4 3 2 1

TO MY HUSBAND, JASON—

Thank you for being my biggest supporter and my best friend. I know that during the year it took to develop this cookbook, a lot of sacrifices were made, and yet you did not complain once. Thank you for always encouraging me to push on, despite the many times I threw in the towel out of sheer frustration. The blog and this book could not have happened without your love and support.

TO MY PARENTS, DAVID AND BECKY—

Thank you for growing my love of food from the very beginning. You both always encouraged me to chase my dreams and to never give up. Thank you for all the opportunities you have given me, and thank you for all the advice, support, and love that you both continually give. I'm the woman I am today because of you two.

Contents

Introduction

I LOVE FOOD AND YOU LOVE FOOD, RIGHT? Let's love food together and start from the beginning. . . .

I've always loved food. I get excited by ingredients, and I love seeing what new and creative dishes I can make out of them. As a child I always chose to watch cooking shows over cartoons (PBS's *Yan Can Cook*, anyone?). I liked watching the host chop up onions, brown meats, and measure out ingredients. I learned kitchen tips and tricks, and I would file them away in my head for use at a later time (and I was so excited when a tip or trick actually worked like it was supposed to).

While growing up, I loved being in the kitchen with my mom, even when I got tasked with washing the potatoes or rinsing the rice. I was thrilled when she let me do something "cool" like stir the pot or sauté garlic and onions. The older I got, the more responsibilities I was given in the kitchen, and I loved it all! I believe that being constantly surrounded by the excitement of preparing food is where I picked up my desire to share that excitement with everyone.

Homemade meals were a thing in our household. Since the very beginning, my mom instilled in me the idea that the best meals are "homemade meals." She wouldn't let my brother and I go to school with just a peanut butter and jelly sandwich. She made it a point to make lunches that would blow our friends' lunches out of the water. Homemade sushi in our lunch boxes? Yup, it happened.

Not only did we have rock star lunches, we would have a home-cooked meal every single night of the week. Looking back, I don't know how my mom and dad were able to work full-time jobs and then come home and prepare amazing dinners for two starving kids. I don't even have kids, and many nights I want to come home and just lie in bed and watch endless amounts of Netflix with Chinese takeout next to me—although my husband might not approve of that. Anyway, the point is my parents didn't find any of this to be a chore, because in the end their efforts provided us with a delicious home-cooked meal and *love*.

Showing someone how much you love him or her through food is the best expression of love I know.

Many of the memories I have are tied to food in one way or another. That correlation between food, love, and memories is at the root of why I started my food blog *Table for Two*. I titled my blog *Table for Two* not for the serving sizes of my recipes but because this title aptly describes the lifestyle that my husband and I enjoy. However, shortly after I started blogging, a number of readers sent me e-mails asking how to cut down a particular recipe for just one or two people, or if I could post more recipes for two. Well, I thought, why not write an entire book on dinner entrées for two?

My cooking mantra has always been quick, easy, and delicious any night of the week. I truly believe this cookbook can help you achieve this too. All the recipes here are pared down for two, and should produce little or no leftovers. The beauty of these recipes is that the ingredient lists aren't complicated; most will probably be in your pantry or freezer! If the ingredients for a recipe require a run to the grocery store, try to prepare a menu plan for the week before going to the store so that you can grab everything in one trip. Making a homemade dinner every night is easier when everything you need is already in your kitchen.

I want to share with everyone my love for food, and I want to show that cooking a delicious home-cooked meal doesn't have to be complicated or fancy. My hope with this cookbook is that you'll get into the kitchen, make some new recipes that will become your favorites, and be inspired to share your love of food with everyone around you!

Julie's Kitchen Tips

INVEST IN SMALLER CASSEROLE DISHES. When cooking for two, you won't need large 8-quart casserole dishes. You will find that 1-, 2-, or even 3-quart casserole dishes are perfect for making many of the dishes described in this book.

A 4-QUART SLOW COOKER IS THE RIGHT SIZE FOR TWO. When I make slow cooker dishes, I use a 4-quart slow cooker because it's the perfect size for our meals. Sure, you can go smaller, but the 4-quart size allows you to cook for a larger crowd when needed.

KOSHER SALT IS YOUR FRIEND. The recipes in this book call for plain kosher salt. When cooking, I use kosher salt (as opposed to table salt) because it provides a fresh and clean taste to food. Table salt, when iodized, can give a dish a metallic flavor; but not only that, the granule size of table salt makes it more potent and strong. The difference between 1 teaspoon of kosher salt and 1 teaspoon of table salt can make or break a dish.

SEASON TO TASTE. Every recipe in this book gives a salt and pepper measurement based on a general taste preference. Of course, these preferences vary for everyone. If you feel a dish needs that extra oomph, by all means add some more salt or pepper or seasonings. Remember that you can always add more seasonings, but you can't take them out, so definitely taste as you go!

GRATE YOUR OWN CHEESE. Yes, it's convenient to grab the pre-shredded stuff, but there's just nothing better than freshly grated cheese. It melts better, does not put that powdery, gritty substance in your dishes, and it ultimately tastes and looks better on all your food!

CHECK YOUR OVEN RACKS. Different heights in the oven yield different results in baked dishes. To yield even baking results, use a rack that is placed in the middle of the oven.

SELECT SMALLER PRODUCE. When cooking for two, you typically don't need a large onion or large bell pepper. Try to select the smaller ones so that you won't have to save them for another night.

HALF A CAN LEFTOVER. It happens: you make a dish but end up using only half a can of diced tomatoes or beans. You may be tempted to toss out the unused portion, but the good news is that the recipes in this book will help you use up that other half of your can.

LEFTOVERS ARE NOT A BAD THING. Even though the recipes in this book were developed for a general serving size of two, it's not always going to happen. For one thing, preferred portion sizes vary, of course. Also, if you add a side salad or bread to the entrées you make, you could have leftovers. You won't have family-sized leftovers, but you might have enough left over to make a great lunch the next day. This is a good thing, because a home-cooked meal is usually much healthier (and cheaper) than café or restaurant fare.

READ THE ENTIRE RECIPE BEFORE DIVING IN. It seems silly to state the obvious, but before you start cooking you should know what ingredients you'll need, when you'll need them, and how much you'll need. If you watch professional chefs in the kitchen or on television, you'll see that they always have the ingredients prepared (measured and chopped) and in order on the counter before they start cooking.

DINNER FOR TWO

Rustic Pot Pie with Biscuits

PREP TIME: 15 MINUTES

COOK TIME: 40 MINUTES

TOTAL TIME: 55 MINUTES

FOR THE BISCUITS

3 tablespoons cold salted butter, cubed

1 cup self-rising flour (see note)

¼ cup + 1 tablespoon milk

FOR THE FILLING

1 tablespoon unsalted butter

½ small onion, diced (about ½ cup)

2 celery ribs, diced

1 garlic clove, minced

1 cup frozen peas and carrots mix, thawed

¾ pound boneless, skinless chicken breasts, cut into 1-inch cubes

1½ tablespoons all-purpose flour

1 cup chicken broth

½ teaspoon kosher salt

¼ teaspoon ground black pepper

Most days I don't have the time to make a pretty crust for a chicken pot pie, so I came up with this rustic recipe. Instead of having a crust, you make the filling for the pot pie, put it in a casserole dish, top it with drop biscuits, and bake it all together. Perfect, right?

· ·

Preheat oven to 425°F. Have a 2-quart, oven-safe casserole dish handy.

Prepare the biscuits: In a small bowl, cut butter into flour with a pastry cutter or a fork until pea-sized crumbs form. Add the milk and stir together with a spatula or wooden spoon until a ball of dough forms (it will be sticky; it's okay), and set aside.

Make the filling: In a skillet over medium-high heat, melt butter. Then add onion, celery, garlic, and peas and carrots mix to the skillet. Sauté until onion and celery have softened, about 5 to 7 minutes. Add the chicken and cook it halfway through, about 3 minutes.

Sprinkle flour on top, and stir around to cook off the raw flour taste, about 2 minutes. Add the chicken broth, salt, and pepper. Let simmer for 10 minutes so mixture can thicken.

Remove from heat and place the filling in a 2-quart casserole dish.

Using a small cookie scoop, scoop the biscuit dough on top of the filling. It doesn't have to be perfect. Just plop it all over the top!

Bake uncovered for 20 minutes and serve warm!

· ·

NOTE: If you don't have self-rising flour, you can use all-purpose flour. Be sure to add 1½ teaspoons baking powder and ¼ teaspoon kosher salt to it.

Parmesan-Crusted Chicken Rice Bowls

Anything that's crusted in cheese is a winner in my book. The crunchy parmesan-crusted chicken atop the bed of rice makes a satisfying dinner for any night of the week!

. . . .

In three shallow dishes, put flour in one dish, the breadcrumbs, garlic powder, salt, pepper, and ¼ cup of Parmesan cheese in another, then the egg in the third dish. Line up the shallow dishes: flour, egg, breadcrumbs.

Gently pound the chicken breasts with a mallet or similar tool until thin.

Heat a large skillet to medium-high heat, and add vegetable oil.

While the pan is heating up, coat one chicken breast on both sides with flour, shaking off the excess, then dip it in the egg, and then coat with the breadcrumb mixture, shaking off the excess. Repeat with the other chicken breast.

Once the skillet is heated, place the chicken breasts into the skillet, brown on both sides, and cook chicken until internal temperature reaches 160°F, about 5 to 7 minutes each side.

Set chicken aside on a plate to cool a bit before slicing into strips, about 5 minutes.

In the meantime, toss rice with parsley and the remaining ¼ cup of Parmesan cheese. If desired, add salt and pepper.

Divide rice between two bowls. Then place chicken strips on top of rice.

PREP TIME: 10 MINUTES
COOK TIME: 20 MINUTES
TOTAL TIME: 30 MINUTES

¼ cup all-purpose flour

¼ cup Italian-seasoned breadcrumbs

½ teaspoon garlic powder

1 teaspoon kosher salt

½ teaspoon ground black pepper

½ cup freshly grated Parmesan cheese

1 large egg, beaten

2 boneless, skinless chicken breasts, pounded thinly

2 tablespoons vegetable oil

1½ cups cooked white rice

2 tablespoons chopped parsley

Salt and pepper to taste

Holy Yum Chicken Kebobs

PREP TIME: 10 MINUTES

COOK TIME: 50 MINUTES

TOTAL TIME: 1 HOUR

²/₃ cup Dijon mustard (like Grey Poupon)

¼ cup + 1 tablespoon pure maple syrup

1 tablespoon plain white vinegar

½ teaspoon kosher salt

¼ teaspoon ground black pepper

1½ pounds chicken breasts, diced into 2-inch cubes

Rosemary sprigs for topping

These kebobs are based on the most popular chicken recipe on my blog, Holy Yum Chicken. The sauce is addictive! If you haven't tried Holy Yum Chicken before, then these kebobs definitely need to be on your menu.

· ·

Soak five wooden skewers on a baking sheet filled with water just enough to cover the skewers. Set aside.

Preheat oven to 425°F, and line a 9 × 13-inch oven-safe casserole dish with two layers of foil. Set aside.

In a small bowl, whisk together mustard, maple syrup, vinegar, salt, and pepper.

Spear 5 or 6 chicken cubes on each wooden skewer.

Place the skewers into the casserole dish. If your skewers are too long, cut or break them to fit the casserole dish.

Pour half the sauce on top of the chicken skewers and, using a pastry brush, brush the sauce to coat the chicken. Set leftover sauce aside.

Place in the oven on the top rack and bake for a total of 45 minutes, uncovered. Flip the chicken skewers every 15 minutes, and brush the chicken with a liberal amount of the leftover sauce until the chicken is cooked fully through (internal temperature of 160°F).

Set oven to broil, and broil chicken for 5 minutes, watching it carefully as not to burn it.

Remove and let cool for 10 minutes before serving.

· ·

NOTE: If you have leftover sauce, use it as a dipping sauce!

We love serving the chicken kebobs with a side of vegetables or white or brown rice.

Ranch Chicken Bacon Burgers

When we make burgers, we usually use beef. But then we discovered ground chicken. It's incredibly moist, and because chicken tastes plain on its own, its potential is so versatile. Layering ground chicken with flavors makes for an outstanding burger!

· ·

Cook the bacon in a medium skillet over medium-high heat to your desired doneness. Reserve bacon fat in the skillet, and drain bacon on a plate lined with paper towels.

In a medium bowl, combine ground chicken, ranch seasoning, breadcrumbs, pepper, and egg. Use your hands to mix it well, making sure everything is incorporated. Do not overmix.

Divide the chicken mixture into two fairly even portions, forming circular patties with your hands.

In the same skillet you used for your bacon, reheat it over medium-high heat. Add one chicken patty to the skillet. Cook until browned on both sides and the patty is cooked through, about 5 minutes each side, or longer depending on thickness. Repeat with the second patty.

To assemble burgers, place a chicken patty on the bottom bun. Top with bacon slices and the top bun. Repeat for the other burger.

· ·

NOTE: Serve with oven-baked french fries, side salad, or potato chips.

PREP TIME: 10 MINUTES
COOK TIME: 15 MINUTES
TOTAL TIME: 25 MINUTES

4 slices bacon

¹/₂ pound ground chicken

1 ounce packet dry ranch seasoning mix

4 tablespoons Italian-seasoned breadcrumbs

¹/₄ teaspoon ground black pepper

1 large egg

2 hamburger buns

Pesto Chicken Salad Sandwich

PREP TIME: 15 MINUTES
COOK TIME: N/A
TOTAL TIME: 15 MINUTES

FOR THE BASIL PESTO

3 cups loosely packed fresh basil leaves

2 tablespoons freshly grated Parmesan cheese

2 tablespoons pine nuts

1 garlic clove

1 teaspoon kosher salt

⅓ cup extra virgin olive oil

FOR THE CHICKEN SALAD

2 cups shredded cooked chicken

⅓ cup fresh basil pesto (above recipe)

¼ cup plain Greek yogurt

2 (6-inch) sub rolls

Sliced tomatoes (optional)

My husband loves chicken salad, but I don't make it often because I'm not a huge fan of mayo. However, after thinking more about chicken salad and how to change it up, this pesto version came to mind. I'm a new fan of chicken salad . . . with pesto, that is.

• •

Make the pesto: In a food processor, add the basil, Parmesan, pine nuts, garlic clove, and salt to the bowl. While the food processor is running, drizzle the olive oil through the feed chute. Scrape down the sides of the bowl, if necessary, and pulse a few times.

Make the chicken salad: In a medium bowl, mix together chicken, pesto, and Greek yogurt until everything is combined and mixed together well.

Divide the chicken mixture between the two sub rolls. Add the tomato slices on top, if using.

20-Minute Teriyaki Chicken and Broccoli

This is the perfect take-out, fake-out dish when you're looking to satisfy your Chinese food craving! Making this dish takes way less time than waiting for the take-out guy to show up, and the sauce has the perfect sweet and savory combination!

. . . .

For the sauce: In a small bowl, whisk together all the ingredients for the sauce and set aside.

For the remainder: Bring a medium pot of water to a boil and add the broccoli. Blanch the broccoli for 5 minutes, then immediately transfer the broccoli to an ice bath (a large bowl of water with ice in it) to stop the cooking process. Set aside.

Heat the oil in a medium skillet over medium-high heat. Brown and cook the chicken for about 5 to 7 minutes. Add the broccoli (drained well), and turn the heat down to medium. Gently pour in the sauce and let thicken, about 5 minutes. Gently toss the ingredients in the sauce until everything is coated well.

Serve over white or brown rice.

. . . .

NOTE: If you're using frozen broccoli, you will not need to blanch it. Make sure you thaw the broccoli and drain it of excess water. Add to the skillet the same time that fresh broccoli would be added.

PREP TIME: 10 MINUTES
COOK TIME: 10 MINUTES
TOTAL TIME: 20 MINUTES

FOR THE SAUCE

2 garlic cloves, minced

1/2 cup low-sodium soy sauce

1/4 cup water

2 tablespoons rice wine vinegar

1/4 cup dark brown sugar

2 tablespoons cornstarch

FOR THE REMAINDER OF THE DISH

4 cups fresh broccoli (see note)

1 tablespoon vegetable oil

1 large boneless, skinless chicken breast, diced into 1-inch cubes

Shredded Chicken Caprese Couscous Bowls

PREP TIME: 10 MINUTES

COOK TIME: 15 MINUTES

TOTAL TIME: 25 MINUTES

1¹⁄₃ cups chicken broth

1¹⁄₃ cups couscous

2 cups cooked
shredded chicken

1 cup freshly shredded
mozzarella cheese

Handful of basil
leaves, julienned

1 teaspoon kosher salt

¹⁄₂ teaspoon ground
black pepper

2 Roma tomatoes,
sliced

Balsamic vinegar
glaze (see note)

A simple and fresh take on a Caprese salad but in a couscous bowl! We love converting and deconstructing classic salads and sandwiches into bowls. Sometimes it's just more filling that way.

. . . .

Bring chicken broth to a boil in a medium pot over medium-high heat. Remove from heat. Add couscous to the pot. Stir, cover, and let sit for 10 minutes. After 10 minutes, use a fork to fluff the couscous.

Place the warm couscous in a large bowl. Add the chicken, mozzarella, basil, salt, and pepper to the bowl. Toss to evenly distribute ingredients.

Divide the couscous into two bowls. Place slices of tomatoes on top, and drizzle with balsamic vinegar glaze.

. . . .

NOTE: If you cannot find balsamic vinegar glaze in your grocery store, you can use regular balsamic vinegar.

Mediterranean Couscous Salad with Grilled Chicken

This is a great dish if you need to empty the refrigerator of leftover ingredients, or if you just want a light and refreshing dinner with bold flavors!

. . . .

Preheat outdoor grill to high. Drizzle vegetable oil on both sides of the chicken. Sprinkle a pinch of the salt and pepper on both sides. Grill the chicken on both sides until the insides reach 160°F. Remove from grill, and set aside to cool. Once cooled, chop into 1-inch cubes.

In a small pot, bring chicken broth to a boil. Remove from heat. Add the couscous to the pot, cover, and let steep for 15 minutes.

Using a fork, fluff the couscous, and place it into a large bowl. Add the tomatoes, cucumber, olives, onion, feta cheese, and chicken.

Drizzle the olive oil on top, and then the lemon juice. Add the remaining salt and pepper, and gently toss everything together.

You can serve this dish warm or chilled. If you prefer chilled, put in the refrigerator for 3 hours before serving.

. . . .

NOTE: If you do not have an outdoor grill, you can easily grill the chicken on an indoor grill or in a regular skillet on the stovetop.

PREP TIME: 10 MINUTES
COOK TIME: 20 MINUTES
TOTAL TIME: 30 MINUTES

1 teaspoon vegetable oil

1 large boneless, skinless chicken breast

1 teaspoon kosher salt, divided

1/2 teaspoon ground black pepper, divided

3/4 cup chicken broth

3/4 cup couscous

1/2 cup halved grape tomatoes

1/2 cucumber, cubed (about 1 cup)

1/2 cup Kalamata olives, roughly chopped

1/2 small red onion, diced (about 1/2 cup)

1 cup crumbled feta cheese

1/4 cup olive oil

Juice of 1/2 lemon

Chicken Lettuce Wraps

PREP TIME: 15 MINUTES
COOK TIME: 10 MINUTES
TOTAL TIME: 25 MINUTES

FOR THE SAUCE

2 tablespoons low-sodium soy sauce

2 tablespoons dark brown sugar

½ teaspoon rice wine vinegar

1½ teaspoons sesame oil

1 tablespoon vegetable oil

FOR THE FILLING

2 teaspoons vegetable oil

½ medium onion, diced (about ¾ cup)

3 garlic cloves, minced

¾ cup water chestnuts, finely chopped

½ cup shiitake mushrooms, finely chopped

1 large cooked boneless, skinless chicken breast, finely chopped (see note)

1 cup cooked white rice

6 large lettuce leaves

If you have ever been to the iconic restaurant P. F. Chang's, where these chicken lettuce wraps originated, then chances are you already know how addictive they are. As much as we love this restaurant dish, we can't justify the price for the small portion, so we make it at home! It tastes just the same, if not better!

· ·

For the sauce: In a small bowl, whisk together all the ingredients for the sauce. Set aside.

For the filling: In a large skillet over medium-high heat, add the vegetable oil. When the oil is hot and glistening, add the onion and garlic cloves. Sauté until translucent and fragrant, about 2 minutes.

Add the water chestnuts, mushrooms, and chicken. Pour the sauce all over the mixture, and stir to combine, making sure everything gets coated with the sauce. Let mixture cook for 5 minutes to warm through, stirring occasionally. Remove the skillet from heat.

To assemble lettuce wraps, place a generous amount of cooked white rice in the bed of each lettuce leaf, then top with chicken mixture. As an optional garnish, sprinkle green onions on top.

· ·

NOTE: I put the chicken breast in boiling water, let it poach for 12 minutes, cool down, and then finely chop it.

Honey Sriracha Lime Chicken Skillet

I love the combination of sweet, salty, and spicy. This chicken dish gives you all that and more. I guarantee you that this is one dish you will be making over and over again. It's so easy and so yummy, and you'll hardly believe it only takes 25 minutes to make.

. . . .

Make the sauce: In a small bowl, whisk together all the ingredients for the sauce and set aside.

Prepare the chicken: In a 10-inch round cast-iron skillet or 10-inch round oven-safe skillet, heat the vegetable oil over medium-high heat.

Preheat the oven to broil.

While the oil is heating up, pat dry the chicken thighs, and sprinkle with salt and pepper on both sides.

Once the oil is hot and glistening, add the chicken to the skillet. Let it get a nice, browned color on one side before turning it, about 3 minutes. Repeat for the other side.

Turn the heat down to medium, and add the sauce on top. Let the sauce and chicken simmer together for 10 minutes, turning occasionally. You'll want to continually baste the chicken with the sauce using a pastry brush.

After simmering, place the entire skillet on the top rack of the oven to broil. Keep an eye on it. It should be done within 5 minutes.

Brush the tops of the chicken with sauce before serving, and add salt and pepper to taste. Serve with rice or your favorite vegetables. The extra sauce will be perfect on top!

. . . .

NOTE: If you prefer to use boneless, skinless chicken breasts, you may do so, but keep in mind that it may yield a dryer dish. I highly recommend using boneless, skinless chicken thighs.

PREP TIME: 5 MINUTES
COOK TIME: 20 MINUTES
TOTAL TIME: 25 MINUTES

FOR THE SAUCE

1/3 cup honey

1 tablespoon Sriracha sauce

1 tablespoon vegetable oil

Juice of 1 lime

1/2 teaspoon kosher salt

1/4 teaspoon ground black pepper

FOR THE CHICKEN

1/2 tablespoon vegetable oil

1 1/4 pounds boneless, skinless chicken thighs

Salt and pepper to season

Skillet Salsa and Cheddar Chicken

'm always looking for ways to jazz up chicken dishes, because we eat a lot of it, and variety is always good. We had a jar of leftover salsa in the fridge, so I decided to experiment and throw it on top of chicken. A whim of an idea turned out to be a dish that is irresistible!

PREP TIME: 5 MINUTES
COOK TIME: 15 MINUTES
TOTAL TIME: 20 MINUTES

- 1½ teaspoons vegetable oil
- 2 large boneless, skinless chicken breasts (see note)
- ½ cup salsa (mild, medium, spicy, chunky, etc.)
- ½ cup freshly grated sharp cheddar cheese
- 2 tablespoons fresh parsley, chopped (optional)

. . . .

Preheat oven to 400°F.

Over medium-high heat in a 10-inch cast-iron skillet or 10-inch round oven-safe skillet, add vegetable oil and brown chicken on both sides, about 2 minutes each side. Remove from heat.

Gently pour ¼ cup of salsa on each chicken breast, and then place the skillet into the oven on the middle rack and bake for 15 minutes or until the insides of the chicken breasts register 160°F.

Remove skillet from oven, and then set the oven to broil. Sprinkle ¼ cup of cheese on top of each chicken breast, and place under broiler for 2 minutes (see note). Remove from oven and sprinkle fresh parsley on top, if desired.

. . . .

NOTES: If you prefer to use boneless, skinless chicken thighs, you may do so.

Continually check on it while it broils. Depending on the thickness of your chicken breast, you may need to cook it longer or shorter.

Buffalo Chicken Pizza

PREP TIME: 20 MINUTES
COOK TIME: 12 MINUTES
TOTAL TIME: 32 MINUTES

FOR THE DOUGH

1 package store-bought pizza dough, or 1 recipe for your homemade dough

FOR THE TOPPING

1 large boneless, skinless chicken breast, cooked and shredded

1/3 cup buffalo sauce

1/4 cup blue cheese dressing

2 tablespoons blue cheese crumbles

I love buffalo chicken anything, especially when it's on a pizza. This combination is the best of both worlds, but the pizza is a bit less messy than wings. Save those hand wipes, and get your hands on a slice or two or three of this pizza!

. . . .

Bring dough to room temperature.

Lightly dust a nonstick, 12-inch pizza pan with flour. Work and stretch the dough to fit the entire pan.

Preheat oven to 500°F.

For the topping: In a medium bowl, toss the shredded chicken in buffalo sauce.

To assemble your pizza, pour the blue cheese dressing on top of the pizza dough. Gently spread it out with a knife or spatula. Add the buffalo chicken on top in an even, thin layer. Sprinkle the blue cheese crumbles on top of the buffalo chicken.

Place pizza on the middle rack in the oven and bake for 11 to 12 minutes or until dough is nice and brown around the edges, the chicken has warmed through, and the cheese is melted.

Let cool for 15 minutes. Slice into wedges and serve.

. . . .

NOTE: Store-bought dough can differ in cooking time and baking temperature depending on the brand. Double-check the packaging for more information.

Slow Cooker Pulled BBQ Chicken Sandwiches

The barbeque sauce for this slow cooker chicken has a trifecta of flavor: sweet, tangy, and a sassy kick of spice! We smother it all over the chicken and then some. This is one of those sandwiches where sauce will be dripping down your hands, but you won't even care, because you're too busy devouring it!

. . . .

For the sauce: In a medium bowl, whisk together all the ingredients for the sauce and set aside.

For the sandwiches: Place the chicken thighs into a slow cooker, and pour the sauce on top of the chicken.

Cook on low for 3 hours.

Once the chicken is completely cooked through, remove it from the slow cooker, and roughly shred it with two forks on a flat surface. Add the shredded chicken back into the slow cooker, and toss it in the sauce to coat.

Spoon a heaping amount of chicken onto two bottom buns, and place the upper buns on top.

Serve with your favorite side dishes or a salad.

. . . .

NOTE: If you prefer to use boneless, skinless chicken breasts, you may do so, but keep in mind that it may yield a dryer dish. I highly recommend using boneless, skinless chicken thighs.

PREP TIME: 5 MINUTES
COOK TIME: 3 HOURS
TOTAL TIME: 3 HOURS, 5 MINUTES

FOR THE SAUCE

¾ cup ketchup

3 tablespoons honey

1½ tablespoons Worcestershire sauce

¼ cup dark brown sugar

1 tablespoon apple cider vinegar

¼ teaspoon garlic powder

¼ teaspoon onion powder

2 teaspoons yellow mustard

FOR THE SANDWICHES

1 pound boneless, skinless chicken thighs (see note)

2 brioche buns, halved

Slow Cooker White Bean and Kielbasa Soup

PREP TIME: 10 MINUTES

COOK TIME: 7 HOURS

TOTAL TIME: 7 HOURS, 10 MINUTES

1 cup (8 ounces) dried great northern beans (or navy beans)

7 ounces kielbasa sausage, sliced into rounds

1/2 onion, diced (about 1/2 cup)

3 cloves garlic, finely minced

2 cups chicken broth

1 (15-ounce) can diced tomatoes, undrained

1/2 teaspoon kosher salt

1/4 teaspoon ground black pepper

4 cups loosely packed baby spinach leaves

I love a good slow cooker recipe. There aren't many slow cooker soups that blow me away, but if I do say so myself, this soup definitely does. The kielbasa is key in this dish because of its smokiness. You'll be scraping the bottom of your bowl wishing for more!

· ·

Place all the ingredients except for the spinach into the slow cooker. Cover and cook on low for 7 hours.

Add spinach to the soup, and stir until the spinach is wilted.

Serve hot with crusty bread on the side for dipping.

Slow Cooker Curry Quinoa Turkey Bowls

My husband and I are huge fans of Indian flavors, and I knew I had to include at least one Indian-inspired dish in this book. The spices are definitely a must, so don't omit them, because they're what give this dish its unique flavors. It is so worth it to find the spices noted here (they're very common, so this shouldn't be a problem)! You'll also love how little work it takes to put this dish together.

. . . .

In a large skillet over medium-high heat, brown ground turkey until cooked through, about 7 to 10 minutes. Add the onions and cook until fragrant, about 5 minutes. Remove from heat.

In the slow cooker, add tomato purée, chicken broth, garam masala, curry powder, turmeric, garbanzo beans, diced tomatoes, quinoa, salt, and pepper. Stir to incorporate all the spices and ingredients.

Carefully add the ground turkey and onion mixture, and stir again to incorporate.

Cover and cook for 3½ hours on high or 6 hours on low.

Divide into bowls and serve. Sprinkle chopped parsley on top, if desired.

PREP TIME: 15 MINUTES
COOK TIME: 3½ HOURS
TOTAL TIME: 3 HOURS,
45 MINUTES

½ pound ground turkey

1 medium onion, diced (about ¾ cup)

1½ cups tomato purée

½ cup chicken broth

1 tablespoon garam masala

1½ tablespoons curry powder

½ teaspoon turmeric powder

1 (15.5-ounce) can garbanzo beans, drained and rinsed

1 (15.5-ounce) can diced tomatoes, undrained

½ cup uncooked quinoa

1½ teaspoons kosher salt

½ teaspoon ground black pepper

Chopped parsley for topping (optional)

Slow Cooker Chicken and Wild Rice Comfort Stew

PREP TIME: 5 MINUTES

COOK TIME: 5 HOURS

TOTAL TIME: 5 HOURS, 5 MINUTES

1 small onion (about ½ cup)

3 celery stalks, diced

2 carrots, diced

¾ cup wild rice blend

¼ teaspoon dried thyme

¼ teaspoon dried oregano

1 teaspoon kosher salt

½ teaspoon ground black pepper

1 chicken bouillon cube (it will dissolve on its own in the slow cooker)

3½ cups chicken broth

1 chicken breast (about ½ pound)

This stew is pure comfort food that warms your soul. It is so easy to make, and you get to come home to the most amazing stew, ever!

• •

Place all the ingredients into the slow cooker and stir around to gently mix everything.

Cook on low for 5 hours.

Remove the chicken and shred with two forks. Place it back into the slow cooker and stir to mix all together.

If the stew is too thick for you, add a bit more chicken broth to thin it out.

Serve warm and with crusty bread, if desired.

Slow Cooker Roasted Lemon and Herb Cornish Hens

These Cornish hens will be calling your name for a date night in! This dish is easy to make, yet it looks like you spent all day on it. The Cornish hens will stay incredibly moist and juicy, though you might have a hard time believing that this dish comes out of a slow cooker!

. . . .

Place potatoes, onion, garlic cloves, and rosemary sprigs into the bottom of the slow cooker.

In a small ramekin, mix together basil, oregano, salt, and pepper.

Gently pat the Cornish hens with a paper towel to absorb any excess liquid. Rub vegetable oil evenly on the outside of the hens and evenly sprinkle spice mixture, gently patting the spices into the skin.

Place one quarter of a lemon into each Cornish hen cavity. Put the remaining lemon quarters into the slow cooker.

Place the Cornish hens onto the bed of vegetables. They should be able to fit side by side.

Cook on high for 3 hours or until internal temperature reaches 160°F.

Remove Cornish hens from slow cooker and place them on a baking sheet to rest for 10 minutes. If you want to crisp up the outer skin, place the Cornish hens under the broiler for 5 to 7 minutes.

Serve Cornish hens with the potatoes and onions. Throw away the garlic, lemon, and rosemary sprigs.

PREP TIME: 10 MINUTES
COOK TIME: 3 HOURS
TOTAL TIME: 3 HOURS,
10 MINUTES

3 small red potatoes, cut into quarters (about 2 cups)

1 small onion, cut into quarters

8 cloves garlic, gently smashed while keeping it mostly whole and outer skin removed

3 stalks of rosemary sprigs

1 teaspoon dried basil

1 teaspoon dried oregano

1 teaspoon kosher salt

½ teaspoon ground black pepper

2 (1½ pound) Cornish hens, rinsed and patted dry, giblets pouches removed

2 teaspoons vegetable oil, divided

1 large lemon, cut into quarters

Creamy Spinach Artichoke Pasta Bake

PREP TIME: 20 MINUTES
COOK TIME: 30 MINUTES
TOTAL TIME: 50 MINUTES

2½ cups dried cavatappi pasta (or any curly pasta)

2 tablespoons unsalted butter

2 tablespoons all-purpose flour

1¼ cups chicken broth

1 garlic clove, minced

2 ounces plain cream cheese, room temperature

½ heaping cup Parmesan cheese

1 teaspoon kosher salt

½ teaspoon ground black pepper

1 (14-ounce) can quartered artichoke hearts, drained

6 cups loosely packed baby spinach

FOR THE TOPPING

2 tablespoons unsalted butter, melted

½ cup panko breadcrumbs

½ cup Parmesan cheese

If you've ever had spinach artichoke dip, you know how sinfully addictive it is. This pasta version is just as addictive, and you'll want it on the regular dinner rotation!

. . . .

Bring a pot of water to a boil, and cook pasta to al dente according to the directions on the package. Drain well when done, and set aside.

Meanwhile, preheat oven to 375°F. Lightly spray an oven-safe 2½- or 3-quart casserole dish with cooking spray.

In a large skillet over medium-high heat, melt butter. Whisk the flour into the butter to create a roux. Continue whisking to cook off the raw flour taste. Add the chicken broth and garlic. Let mixture thicken, about 3 minutes. Add the cream cheese, Parmesan, salt, and pepper.

Continue stirring until the cheeses have melted and the mixture is smooth and thick. Add the artichoke hearts and spinach. Stir until the spinach has wilted. Remove from heat.

Add the drained pasta to the skillet, and gently toss to coat the pasta evenly with the sauce.

Pour the pasta into the prepared casserole dish.

In a small bowl, mix together the ingredients for the topping, and sprinkle evenly over the top of the casserole dish.

Bake uncovered for 30 minutes or until top is browned and mixture is bubbly.

Serve warm.

Great-Grandma's Pasta Sauce with Orecchiette

I have a deep love for Italian food. A perk of being married to a half-Italian man is that I get to enjoy his Italian grandmother's authentic Italian dishes! This pasta sauce recipe has been passed down from generation to generation and although we've added our own little tweaks to it, it is still just as good as grandma used to make!

• •

Bring a large pot of water to a boil. Add the orecchiette to the pot, and cook pasta according to instructions on the package. When pasta is done, drain well and set aside.

In a medium pot over medium-high heat, add olive oil. When the oil is hot and glistening, add the garlic, and sauté for 30 seconds or until fragrant. Add the ground beef and break it up with a wooden spoon or spatula. Cook beef until most of the meat is cooked through, about 5 to 7 minutes.

Add the remaining ingredients to the pot. Stir, cover, and turn down the heat to medium-low. Let the mixture simmer, covered, for 30 minutes. Remove the lid and let simmer for another 15 minutes.

To serve, divide pasta into two bowls, and ladle the sauce over the pasta.

PREP TIME: 5 MINUTES
COOK TIME: 1 HOUR
TOTAL TIME: 1 HOUR,
5 MINUTES

2¼ cups dried orecchiette pasta

1 tablespoon olive oil

3 cloves of garlic, minced

½ pound 80/20 ground beef

4 tablespoons tomato paste

1⅔ cups tomato purée

1 tablespoon granulated sugar

¼ teaspoon dried oregano

¼ teaspoon dried basil

¼ teaspoon onion powder

¼ teaspoon garlic powder

½ teaspoon kosher salt

Generous pinch ground black pepper

Spinach Lasagna Roll-Ups

PREP TIME: 20 MINUTES
COOK TIME: 30 MINUTES
TOTAL TIME: 50 MINUTES

FOR THE FILLING

1⅓ cups part-skim ricotta cheese

1 cup mozzarella cheese, divided

¾ cup frozen spinach, thawed and drained of excess liquid

½ teaspoon kosher salt

¼ teaspoon ground black pepper

FOR THE REMAINDER OF DISH

1 cup marinara sauce

½ teaspoon dried basil

½ teaspoon dried oregano

¼ teaspoon garlic powder

¼ teaspoon crushed red pepper flakes (optional)

8 lasagna noodles, cooked (see note)

We love lasagna, but we don't like making an entire casserole and eating leftovers for days on end. Lasagna roll-ups are a *great* alternative because you can easily make the perfect portion for the two of you! Use your favorite marinara for the sauce.

• •

Preheat oven to 350°F.

For the filling: In a medium bowl, combine all the filling ingredients (using only ½ cup of the mozzarella and setting aside the remainder). Stir together with a spoon to incorporate.

For the remainder: In a small bowl, whisk together the marinara sauce and spices.

Spread ⅔ cup of marinara sauce mixture in a thin layer on the bottom of a 2-quart rectangular baking dish. Set aside.

To assemble the lasagna roll-ups, lay a lasagna noodle on a flat surface. Using a ¼ cup measuring cup, scoop out the filling and place it at one of the short ends of the lasagna noodle. Using your fingers, gently press the mixture in a thin, even layer across the entire lasagna noodle. Once the entire noodle is covered with the mixture, gently roll up the noodle, starting from one end of the lasagna noodle on the short side. Do not press too hard.

Place the lasagna roll-up, seam side down, in the prepared baking dish, and repeat until all the lasagna noodles are filled.

Pour the remaining ⅓ cup of marinara sauce over the tops of the lasagna roll-ups. Sprinkle the remaining ½ cup of mozzarella cheese on top.

Loosely cover the baking dish with aluminum foil, and bake for 15 minutes. Remove foil, then bake for another 15 minutes.

• •

NOTE: Quickly cool lasagna noodles by putting them in cold water so they're easier to handle.

Sloppy Joe Mac 'n' Cheese

I f there were ever a dish that I wanted you to drop every-thing to go make, this would be the one. The simplicity of making this dish, plus how outrageously awesome it tastes, makes this a perfect dish to put on rotation! Personally, I think it's better than the traditional sandwich.

. . . .

For the sauce: In a medium bowl, whisk together all the ingredients for the sauce, and set aside.

For the pasta and remainder of dish: Bring a large pot of water to a boil, and cook the pasta according to directions on the package.

In a large skillet over medium-high heat, heat up the vegetable oil. Add the onion, green bell pepper, and garlic. Sauté until fragrant and softened, about 5 minutes.

Add the ground beef to the skillet and break it up with your spatula or wooden spoon. Cook until ground beef is thoroughly cooked through, about 5 to 7 minutes.

Add the sauce to the skillet. Then add the pasta (drained of excess water), and the cheese on top. Turn the heat down to medium-low, and toss the mixture until the cheese has melted and the ingredients are evenly coated and distributed throughout.

Serve warm.

PREP TIME: 5 MINUTES
COOK TIME: 20 MINUTES
TOTAL TIME: 25 MINUTES

FOR THE SAUCE

¾ cup tomato sauce

1 tablespoon tomato paste

2 teaspoons Worcestershire sauce

2 tablespoons dark brown sugar

½ teaspoon kosher salt

¼ teaspoon ground black pepper

FOR THE PASTA AND REMAINDER OF DISH

2 cups rotini (or any spiral-shaped) pasta

1 tablespoon vegetable oil

½ large onion, diced (about ¾ cup)

1 medium green bell pepper, diced (about ½ cup)

2 cloves garlic, minced

½ pound ground beef

1 cup freshly grated sharp cheddar cheese

Roasted Tomatillo and Ranch Chicken Stuffed Shells

PREP TIME: 25 MINUTES
COOK TIME: 20 MINUTES
TOTAL TIME: 45 MINUTES

FOR THE TOMATILLO RANCH SAUCE

½ pound tomatillos, husks removed and halved

1 tablespoon vegetable oil

⅓ cup + 2 tablespoons mayonnaise

¼ cup + 2 tablespoons sour cream

1 (1-ounce) packet ranch seasoning mix

⅓ cup buttermilk

1 teaspoon kosher salt

FOR THE PASTA AND FILLING

10 jumbo pasta shells

⅔ cup part-skim ricotta cheese

⅓ cup freshly grated mozzarella cheese, plus more for topping

½ pound boneless, skinless chicken breast, shredded

Not everything that's delicious looks pretty. That's just a fact of life. Take this dish, for example. Not much pop of color for your eyes, but lots of pop of flavor in your mouth.

. . . .

For the sauce: Preheat oven to broil.

Toss the tomatillos in vegetable oil on a baking sheet. Broil the tomatillos on the middle rack in the oven for 10 minutes or until softened and outside skin is browned. Carefully place tomatillos into blender or food processor.

Turn oven down to 350°F. In a medium bowl, whisk together mayonnaise, sour cream, ranch seasoning mix, buttermilk, and salt. Pour mixture on top of tomatillos in the blender. Blend until mixture is smooth. Pour into a bowl and set aside.

For the pasta and filling: Bring a medium pot of water to a boil, and cook jumbo pasta shells until al dente. Once cooked, place the shells in a bowl of cold water. Set aside.

In another medium bowl, stir together ricotta cheese, mozzarella cheese, and shredded chicken. Add ½ cup of the tomatillo ranch mixture to the ricotta mixture, and stir to incorporate.

Add a thin layer of the tomatillo ranch mixture to the bottom of a 2-quart oven-safe casserole dish.

Pat the pasta shells dry, and place on a plate for easy access.

To stuff the shells: Scoop a heaping tablespoon of filling and place it into the pasta shell. Place the pasta shell into the prepared casserole dish. Repeat until all the shells have been filled and all the filling is used.

Pour the remaining tomatillo ranch sauce on top of the shells and top with additional mozzarella cheese.

Bake uncovered for 20 minutes or until cheese is melted and filling is warmed through. Let cool for 5 minutes before serving.

Thai Peanut Curry Noodle Stir Fry

'm always looking for different Thai-inspired dishes for dinner. Whenever my husband and I go to our favorite Thai restaurant, we notice that peanut sauce and curry are recurring themes. I decided to combine the two, and the result is a noodle dish with wonderful flavors!

· ·

For the sauce: In a medium bowl, whisk together the ingredients for the curry sauce and set aside.

For the remainder: Soak the rice noodles in a large bowl filled with hot tap water. You'll need to soak it for 15 to 20 minutes or until the noodles are softened. Drain and set aside.

In a large skillet over medium-high heat, add the vegetable oil. Once the oil is hot, add the onion and garlic cloves. Cook until softened and fragrant, about 4 minutes.

Add the eggs to the skillet and quickly scramble them together with the onion and garlic. Add the rice noodles to the skillet and turn the heat down to medium-low. Pour the curry sauce all over the noodles. Toss until everything is coated.

Remove from heat and serve. Top with green onions or scallions, if using.

· ·

NOTE: Conventional peanut butter works better in this dish, because natural peanut butter separates and is generally harder to work with due to the stirring and remnant clumpy chunks. Conventional peanut butter is smoother and will yield better results for the sauce.

PREP TIME: 25 MINUTES
COOK TIME: 15 MINUTES
TOTAL TIME: 40 MINUTES

FOR THE CURRY SAUCE

4 tablespoons peanut butter (not natural peanut butter, see note)

3 teaspoons red curry paste

$1/2$ cup sweetened coconut milk

$1/4$ cup water

FOR THE REMAINDER OF THE DISH

10 ounces rice noodles

2 tablespoons vegetable oil

1 medium onion, diced (about $3/4$ cup)

2 garlic cloves, minced

3 large eggs

Green onions or scallions (optional)

Chorizo, Roasted Red Pepper, and Spinach Gnocchi

PREP TIME: 10 MINUTES
COOK TIME: 10 MINUTES
TOTAL TIME: 20 MINUTES

- 16 ounces potato gnocchi
- ½ pound fresh chorizo sausage, casings removed
- ¾ cup chopped, jarred, roasted red peppers
- 1 small onion, chopped (about ½ cup)
- ½ teaspoon kosher salt
- 3 cups loosely packed baby spinach leaves

always forget about gnocchi when making pasta dishes or thinking of dinner. This is a shame, because gnocchi is *so* versatile. It's incredibly easy to throw this dish together using gnocchi, and you'll love how flavorful it is! It's got a great spicy kick that contrasts well with the pillowy gnocchi.

. . . .

Bring a pot of water to boil. Add the gnocchi, and cook it per the instructions on the package.

In a large skillet over medium-high heat, brown chorizo sausage and break it up with a wooden spoon or spatula. Add the roasted red peppers, onions, and salt. Cook until the onions have softened, about 5 to 7 minutes. Add the baby spinach and toss until leaves have wilted.

Drain and add the gnocchi and toss everything to incorporate.

Serve and enjoy.

Cheesy Baked Italian Sausage Tortellini

feel like tortellini is one of those pastas that gets a bad rap, because it's typically premade. This cheesy, baked tortellini goes to show that even if pasta is premade, you can still make it your own with very simple ingredients!

· ·

Preheat oven to 350°F.

In a small pot over medium heat, add marinara sauce, red pepper flakes, and spinach. Cook until spinach has wilted and sauce is warmed through. Remove from heat.

Pour 1/2 of the sauce onto the bottom of a 2 1/2-quart, oven-safe casserole dish. Add the tortellini on top of the sauce. Sprinkle half the cheese on top.

Pour the remaining sauce on top of the cheese layer, then top with the remaining cheese.

Cover casserole dish with foil. Place on the middle rack in the oven, and bake for 60 minutes. In the last 15 minutes of baking, remove the foil to let cheese melt and brown on top.

Remove from oven, let cool for 10 minutes, and then serve.

PREP TIME: 5 MINUTES
COOK TIME: 1 HOUR
TOTAL TIME: 1 HOUR,
5 MINUTES

3 cups (24 ounces) marinara sauce

1/2 teaspoon red pepper flakes

2 cups loosely packed, baby spinach leaves

18 ounces refrigerated sausage tortellini pasta

1 2/3 cups shredded, smoked Gouda cheese

PREP TIME: 10 MINUTES
COOK TIME: 25 MINUTES
TOTAL TIME: 35 MINUTES

FOR THE SUN-DRIED TOMATO PESTO

²/₃ cup julienned sun-dried tomatoes in olive oil, drained, reserving the olive oil

1 garlic clove

2 tablespoons freshly grated Parmesan cheese

FOR THE PASTA AND REMAINDER OF DISH

6 ounces fresh Italian sausage, casings removed

1 cup dried orzo pasta

2 cups chicken broth

1 (14.5 ounce) can quartered artichoke hearts, drained

¼ cup freshly grated Parmesan cheese

1 teaspoon kosher salt

Handful of basil, finely chopped

One-Pot Sun-Dried Tomato Pesto Orzo with Artichokes and Sausage

'm pretty obsessed with sun-dried tomatoes. Making a pesto out of sun-dried tomatoes is one of my favorite things to do when I'm trying to come up with something interesting for dinner. This one ingredient just makes a dish that much more flavorful and unique!

. . . .

For the pesto: In the bowl of a small food processor, add the ingredients for the sun-dried tomato pesto. Drizzle about 2 tablespoons of the reserved olive oil from the tomatoes into the bowl. Process until everything is finely chopped. Set aside.

For the pasta and remainder of dish: In a large skillet, over medium-high heat, brown Italian sausage, and break it up with your wooden spoon or spatula. Add the orzo and stir around to toast. Add the sun-dried tomato pesto and slowly add the chicken broth.

Cover skillet, and turn the heat down to medium-low. Let simmer, stirring occasionally, until orzo has absorbed all the liquid and is cooked through, about 20 minutes.

Add the drained artichoke hearts and cheese to the skillet, and gently toss to incorporate. Add the salt and chopped basil. Toss again to incorporate.

Remove from heat, divide into two bowls, and enjoy.

Roasted Red Pepper Cream Pasta

Making sauces from roasted red peppers is a great way to change up your dinner menu. We love the sweetness of the red peppers, which gives this pasta dish its unique flavor. Don't be surprised if this dish becomes a welcomed addition to your weekly menu!

· ·

Bring a large pot of water to a boil and add the spaghetti pasta to the pot. Cook according to directions on the package. Drain well.

While the spaghetti is cooking, in the bowl of a food processor, add the roasted red bell peppers. Process until red bell peppers are very finely chopped. Set aside.

In a large skillet over medium-high heat, add vegetable oil. When the oil is hot, add the onion and garlic, and sauté for 5 minutes.

Add the processed red bell peppers, Parmesan cheese, chicken broth, and salt to the skillet. Stir to incorporate, and let simmer over medium-low heat for 5 minutes.

Remove skillet from heat and add the cooked spaghetti pasta to the skillet. Using tongs, toss the pasta with the red pepper mixture until all the noodles are coated. Top with fresh basil leaves, if desired.

PREP TIME: 10 MINUTES

COOK TIME: 15 MINUTES

TOTAL TIME: 25 MINUTES

½ pound dried spaghetti pasta

3 large roasted red bell peppers from a jar, liquid drained

1 teaspoon vegetable oil

1 small onion, diced (about ½ cup)

2 garlic cloves, minced

⅓ cup freshly grated Parmesan cheese

¼ cup chicken broth

½ teaspoon kosher salt

Basil leaves for topping (optional)

Creamy Sun-Dried Tomato Fettuccine

PREP TIME: 5 MINUTES

COOK TIME: 25 MINUTES

TOTAL TIME: 30 MINUTES

½ pound dried fettuccine

⅓ cup plain Greek yogurt

¼ cup sour cream

1 tablespoon olive oil

2 garlic cloves, minced

½ cup canned, diced tomatoes, liquid drained

1 tablespoon tomato paste

1 cup marinara sauce

⅓ cup sun-dried tomato halves, chopped

¼ cup frozen spinach, thawed and drained of excess liquid

A restaurant I went to with a friend inspired me to make this pasta dish. The description on the menu made it sound amazing. Amazing it was, but my waistline wasn't happy with me afterward. I re-created this dish to make it slightly lighter. The result is a recipe that has become one of the most popular on my blog. I think it tastes even better than the restaurant version!

. . . .

Bring a large pot of water to a boil and add the dried fettuccine to the pot. Cook according to the directions on the package.

In a small bowl, stir together yogurt and sour cream. Set aside.

In a large skillet over medium heat, add the olive oil. When oil is hot and glistening, add garlic and sauté until fragrant, about 1 minute. Remove skillet from heat, and let cool for 10 minutes (see note).

In the cooled skillet, slowly add the yogurt and sour cream mixture, stirring vigorously as you add it.

Return the skillet to a medium heat, and add diced tomatoes, tomato paste, marinara sauce, and sun-dried tomato halves. Let mixture simmer and thicken, about 5 minutes; then add the frozen spinach, and stir to evenly distribute.

Remove skillet from heat and add the cooked fettuccine. Evenly toss the fettuccine in the sauce until all the pasta is nicely coated.

. . . .

NOTE: Letting the skillet cool for 10 minutes is imperative; otherwise your mixture may curdle due to the high heat retained in the skillet from sautéing the garlic.

Garlic Butter Shrimp Pasta

Seafood dinners always remind me of fancy dinner parties. So why not make this dish and pretend to throw one of your own? Pop a bottle of wine or your favorite drink, and toast to a fancy dinner party with your special person!

PREP TIME: 10 MINUTES
COOK TIME: 20 MINUTES
TOTAL TIME: 30 MINUTES

- 1/2 pound dried linguine pasta
- 1/2 pound jumbo shrimp, shelled and deveined
- 1 teaspoon kosher salt
- 1/4 teaspoon ground black pepper
- 2 tablespoons all-purpose flour, divided
- 2 tablespoons unsalted butter, divided
- 6 garlic cloves, finely minced
- 1/2 cup chicken broth
- 1/4 cup heavy cream

Bring a large pot of water to a boil and cook linguine pasta according to the directions on the package. Drain well.

Meanwhile, toss shrimp in a medium bowl with salt, pepper, and 1 1/2 tablespoons of the flour. Make sure both sides of the shrimp are coated.

In a large skillet over medium-high heat, melt 1 tablespoon of the butter in the pan. Add shrimp to the pan, and cook for 2 to 3 minutes on one side or until they're nice and browned. Flip and cook the other side. Shrimp are done when they're no longer translucent and the outside is bright pink. Remove cooked shrimp from pan and set aside on a plate.

In the same skillet, melt the remaining 1 tablespoon butter. Add the garlic, and sauté for 1 minute or until fragrant.

Add the chicken broth and heavy cream. Whisk in remaining 1/2 tablespoon of flour until all is dissolved. Let mixture simmer and thicken for 5 minutes, stirring occasionally.

Add the cooked pasta to the skillet. Toss with the garlic sauce, and remove from heat. Add the shrimp, and toss to make sure they get well coated with sauce. Season with more salt and pepper to taste, if desired.

Serve warm.

One-Pot Jambalaya

PREP TIME: 15 MINUTES
COOK TIME: 30 MINUTES
TOTAL TIME: 45 MINUTES

1 tablespoon vegetable oil

1 green bell pepper, diced (about 1 cup)

1 small onion, diced (about ½ cup)

2 celery ribs, diced

2 garlic cloves, minced

½ pound boneless, skinless chicken breasts, cut into 1-inch cubes

6 ounces andouille sausage, cut into rounds

1 tablespoon tomato paste

¾ cup long grain white rice

1½ cups chicken broth

1 cup diced tomatoes, undrained

1 tablespoon Cajun seasoning

1 bay leaf

You don't have to travel to Cajun country to get jambalaya! You can easily make it at home for dinner. Best of all, it's a one-pot meal, so the cleanup is a breeze. More time to enjoy your evening. Win-win.

· ·

Add vegetable oil to a large pot or Dutch oven over medium-high heat. When the oil is hot, add the bell pepper, onion, celery, and garlic to the pot. Cook until fragrant, about 3 minutes.

Add the chicken, andouille, and tomato paste. Stir around to mix with the other ingredients and break up the tomato paste.

Add the white rice and stir it around until lightly toasted.

Stir in the chicken broth, diced tomatoes, Cajun seasoning, and bay leaf.

Cover and let cook over low heat for 30 minutes, or until rice is cooked through and the liquid has been completely absorbed. Stir every 10 minutes or so to prevent the rice from sticking to the bottom of the pan.

Serve hot.

Seafood Paella

Paella is a traditional Spanish rice dish that originates from the Valencia region. We're huge fans of paella because it bursts with loads of flavor.

• •

In a small pot over medium-high heat, bring seafood stock and saffron to a boil. Keep over low heat as you prepare the rest of the dish.

Add white wine to a large skillet over medium-high heat. Add half the minced garlic to the skillet and then add the mussels and clams. Cover skillet and let steam for 7 minutes, or until most of the mussels and clams open up. Remove mussels and clams from skillet and place on a plate. Reserve the liquid in the skillet by pouring it into a glass measuring cup. Discard any mussels or clams that did not open up.

In the same large skillet or a paella pan, heat up vegetable oil over medium-high heat and add the remaining minced garlic, onion, and red bell pepper. Sauté for 3 minutes.

Add the canned, fire-roasted diced tomatoes to the skillet. Stir to incorporate, and cook for 5 minutes. Sprinkle paprika and salt over the mixture and stir to combine.

Gently remove the seafood stock and saffron from heat, and pour into the large skillet or paella pan. Add the reserved liquid from the glass measuring cup and stir to incorporate. Bring mixture to a boil. Sprinkle rice into an even layer, do not stir.

Let mixture boil for 5 minutes; then turn down the heat to medium, and let simmer for 20 minutes, or until all the liquid has been absorbed by the rice and the rice is tender. Add more seafood stock if necessary.

Once the liquid has been absorbed by the rice, add in the shrimp, and toss together with the rice until shrimp turns pink and has cooked through, about 5 minutes.

To assemble paella, place rice mixture into a bowl, then place mussels and clams on top. Add some lemon slices, if desired. Serve warm.

PREP TIME: 15 MINUTES
COOK TIME: 35 MINUTES
TOTAL TIME: 50 MINUTES

2½ cups seafood stock or broth

Pinch of saffron

½ cup dry white wine

4 cloves garlic, minced, divided

1 dozen mussels, cleaned and beards removed

1 dozen littleneck clams, cleaned

1 tablespoon vegetable oil

½ medium onion, diced (about ¾ cup)

1 small red bell pepper, diced (about ½ cup)

½ cup canned fire-roasted, diced tomatoes, liquid drained

1 teaspoon sweet paprika

1 teaspoon kosher salt

1 cup bomba paella rice or arborio rice

1 dozen shrimp, with shells

Bulgogi Kimchi Rice Plate

've grown really fond of Korean food lately, so I just had to feature in this book one of the most popular Korean dishes: bulgogi. If you've never had bulgogi before, you're in for a treat!

PREP TIME: 8 HOURS
COOK TIME: 15 MINUTES
TOTAL TIME: 8 HOURS
15 MINUTES

12 ounces thinly sliced
rib eye beef

1 medium onion, sliced

2 garlic cloves, minced

¼ cup soy sauce

1 teaspoon sesame oil

2 tablespoons
granulated sugar

Kimchi, for topping

White or brown rice

Place the rib eye, onion, and garlic into a gallon-sized plastic bag.

In a small bowl, whisk together soy sauce, sesame oil, and granulated sugar.

Pour the soy sauce mixture over the rib eye mixture in the plastic bag. Seal the bag and shake it around, massaging the soy sauce mixture all over the contents of the plastic bag.

Place in refrigerator for 8 hours.

In a large skillet over medium-high heat, pour all the contents of the plastic bag, and cook until meat is done and the onions are tender, about 5 to 7 minutes.

Serve over a bed of white or brown rice and add a generous amount of kimchi on top.

Cheesy Pumpkin Sage Farro with Mushrooms

Cooking with pumpkin in a savory dish is so under-rated. I want to start a "cook more with pumpkin" movement, because there's so much you can do with pumpkin. It's more than dessert! Pumpkin makes a dish so creamy and earthy. And if you've never had farro before, you'll love it—it's an ancient grain that you'll want in your pantry all the time.

· ·

Add farro to a pot of boiling water. Reduce the heat to low, cover the pot, and let farro cook for 20 minutes. If it still has a bite to it and not softened, cook for a bit longer, roughly 10 more minutes. Some liquid might still remain in the pot, which is okay.

Stir in the pumpkin purée. Add the mushrooms. Turn the heat up to medium and let the mushrooms cook until softened, about 10 to 12 minutes.

Add the cheese, salt, pepper, and sage. Stir until cheese has melted.

Serve warm.

· ·

NOTE: Farro can also be bought in a "quick" version that doesn't need to cook for 20 minutes. If you have the quick version, refer to the directions on the package for cooking.

PREP TIME: 5 MINUTES
COOK TIME: 30 MINUTES
TOTAL TIME: 35 MINUTES

1 cup farro

2½ cups water

⅔ cup pumpkin purée (not pumpkin pie filling)

2 cups sliced portobello mushrooms

1 cup grated Parmesan cheese

1 teaspoon kosher salt

¼ teaspoon ground black pepper

1 large sage leaf (or two small), finely chopped

Beef Enchilada Rice Bake

PREP TIME: 10 MINUTES
COOK TIME: 30 MINUTES
TOTAL TIME: 40 MINUTES

2 teaspoons vegetable oil

1 medium onion, diced (about ¾ cup)

1 green bell pepper, diced (about ¾ cup)

1 garlic clove, minced

1 teaspoon ground cumin

1 teaspoon kosher salt

½ teaspoon ground black pepper

½ pound 80/20 ground beef

1 (10-ounce) can diced tomatoes and green chilies, drained well

2 cups cooked white rice

½ cup red enchilada sauce, plus more for drizzling

1½ cups shredded Mexican cheese

Mexican flavors are huge in our household. They're so versatile! In this recipe, I take the classic beef enchilada and convert it into a rice bake! As a result, all the flavors of a classic enchilada are there but without the heating up and assembly of the tortillas.

· ·

Preheat oven to 375°F.

In a large skillet over medium-high heat, add the vegetable oil. Once the oil is heated up, add onion, green bell pepper, and garlic. Sauté for 5 minutes. Sprinkle in cumin, salt, and black pepper. Stir to incorporate.

Place beef into the skillet and break it up into pieces with a wooden spoon or spatula.

Add the diced tomatoes and stir to incorporate.

Remove skillet from heat and add the rice to the skillet. Stir rice and beef mixture until evenly distributed. Add the enchilada sauce and stir to incorporate.

Place mixture into a 2½-quart, oven-safe casserole dish. Sprinkle cheese evenly on top of the rice.

Place the casserole dish in the oven on the middle rack, and bake, uncovered, for 20 minutes.

Carefully remove from the oven and drizzle more enchilada sauce on top, if desired.

Roasted Vegetable Couscous with Pan-Seared Scallops

There is something magical that happens when you roast vegetables, and this dish incorporates that magical goodness with deliciously plump scallops on top of pearl couscous.

. . . .

Preheat oven to 425°F.

Lightly spray a baking sheet with cooking spray. Set aside.

In a large bowl, add the zucchini, carrots, tomatoes, and broccoli. Drizzle olive oil over the vegetables and season with 1 teaspoon salt and 1/4 teaspoon black pepper. Using a spatula, toss vegetables to coat.

Pour the vegetables onto the prepared baking sheet in an even layer. Bake for 40 minutes on the middle rack, rotating the pan halfway through baking and flipping the vegetables with a spatula. Remove from oven and set aside.

Meanwhile, bring a medium pot of water to a boil. Add the pearl couscous to the pot and cook according to instructions on the package. Remove from heat and set aside.

Add 1 teaspoon of vegetable oil to a small skillet over medium-high heat.

Sprinkle remaining salt and pepper evenly over tops of the scallops and place four scallops, seasoned side down, into the hot skillet. Do not move the scallops. Let scallops sear for 3 minutes or until browned. Flip the scallops and cook for another 3 minutes. Remove, and set aside on a plate. Add the remaining 1 teaspoon of vegetable oil to the skillet and repeat the cooking process for the remaining four scallops.

In a large bowl, add the cooked couscous and roasted vegetables. Using a spatula, gently toss the ingredients together.

Evenly divide couscous mixture and scallops into two bowls.

PREP TIME: 10 MINUTES
COOK TIME: 1 HOUR
TOTAL TIME: 1 HOUR,
10 MINUTES

1 medium zucchini, cut into half-moons

1/2 large carrot, cut into 1/2-inch thick circles

1/2 pint grape tomatoes, sliced in half

2 cups broccoli florets

2 tablespoons olive oil

2 teaspoons kosher salt, divided

3/4 teaspoon ground black pepper, divided

1 cup pearl couscous

2 teaspoons vegetable oil, divided

8 large (1/2 pound total weight) scallops

Kimchi Fried Rice

PREP TIME: 10 MINUTES
COOK TIME: 15 MINUTES
TOTAL TIME: 25 MINUTES

1 tablespoon vegetable oil, divided

2 large eggs

1 small onion, diced (about 1/2 cup)

1 cup frozen vegetables (peas, carrots, corn, or others), thawed

1 clove garlic, finely minced

1 1/2 cups kimchi, roughly chopped

1 tablespoon kimchi juice

3 cups day-old, cooked white rice

1 teaspoon kosher salt

1/2 teaspoon ground black pepper

'm all about changing up the ordinary. I added kimchi into this traditional rice dish to amp up the flavors and kick it up a notch. I think this is our new favorite way to make fried rice!

· ·

In a large skillet over medium-high heat, add 1/2 tablespoon vegetable oil. Once the oil is hot, add the eggs to skillet and scramble them. Remove the scrambled eggs from the skillet, and set aside in a bowl.

Add the remaining 1/2 tablespoon vegetable oil, onion, frozen vegetables, garlic, kimchi, and kimchi juice. Sauté until onion is translucent and cooked through, about 3 minutes.

Add the rice to the skillet and carefully break it up with your spatula or wooden spoon.

Turn the heat down to medium-low, and continue to stir the rice into the mixture until all is incorporated. Finally, add the scrambled eggs and season with salt and pepper.

Serve immediately.

· ·

NOTE: For an even more authentic and spicier kick, add 1 tablespoon of gojuchang paste. Gojuchang paste can be found at Asian grocery stores in the Korean section, or in the Asian aisle at your local grocery store.

Pork Chops with Mushroom, Onion, and Rosemary Cream Sauce

I love this dish for a variety of reasons, but mainly because it's one of those dishes that seems to be time-consuming to prepare but, in fact, it isn't. This dish is simple elegance at its finest. You don't have to reveal how long it actually took you to make this meal. I promise I won't tell!

. . . .

Add olive oil to a large skillet over medium-high heat.

Season both sides of pork chops with salt and pepper.

Place pork chops into sizzling hot skillet and brown both sides but do not cook them all the way through. They cook rather quickly because of their thinness, so be careful. Place on a plate and set aside.

In the same skillet over medium heat, add onion, garlic, and mushrooms. Sauté until onions and mushrooms have softened, about 5 to 7 minutes. Add the white wine and cook until most of the alcohol has evaporated, about 5 minutes.

Sprinkle flour on top of the mushroom and onion mixture, toss, and then add the vegetable broth and heavy cream. Sprinkle in the rosemary and let simmer and thicken for 8 minutes.

Add the pork chops back into the cream sauce and let cook until the pork chops are cooked through, about 5 minutes.

Serve pork chops with the mushroom-onion mixture on top and with your favorite side dish (mashed potatoes, side salad, etc.).

PREP TIME: 10 MINUTES
COOK TIME: 25 MINUTES
TOTAL TIME: 35 MINUTES

½ tablespoon olive oil

6 thinly sliced pork chops, about 1 pound

1 teaspoon kosher salt

½ teaspoon ground black pepper

1 small onion, sliced into half-moons

2 garlic cloves, minced

2 cups sliced portobello mushrooms

¼ cup white wine

1 tablespoon all-purpose flour

¼ cup vegetable broth

1 tablespoon heavy cream

½ tablespoon chopped fresh rosemary

Red Wine Braised Lamb Shank with Mashed Cauliflower

PREP TIME: 10 MINUTES

COOK TIME: 2 HOURS,
15 MINUTES

TOTAL TIME: 2 HOURS,
25 MINUTES

1 tablespoon olive oil

2 lamb shanks (about
1¾ pounds total
weight)

1 large onion, sliced
into half-rings

4 garlic cloves, lightly
smashed

1½ cups dark red wine
(such as cabernet
sauvignon)

1 cup beef broth

3 tablespoons dark
brown sugar

1 tablespoon balsamic
vinegar

¼ teaspoon dry thyme

1 (16-ounce) bag frozen
cauliflower florets

1 tablespoon milk

2 teaspoons arrowroot
powder (or similar,
such as cornstarch)

Braises are some of my favorite comfort dishes. I love how the meat just falls apart at the end of cooking and how all the flavors and juices get cozy with each other. This lamb shank is deliciously tender, and the red wine ends up being a great sweet note to this savory dish.

. . . .

Add olive oil to a large, heavy-bottom pot, such as a Dutch oven, over medium-high heat. Once oil is hot and glistening, brown lamb shanks on all sides. Remove and set aside.

In the same pot, add onions and garlic and sauté until fragrant, about 5 minutes.

Add red wine, beef broth, brown sugar, balsamic vinegar, and thyme to the pot, and stir to incorporate. Place the lamb shanks back into the pot, cover, and let simmer for 2 hours on medium-low heat. About halfway through the cooking process, flip the lamb shanks and stir the liquid.

When the lamb shanks are nearly done, bring a small pot of water to a boil, and add the cauliflower florets to the pot. Cook until florets are tender and soft enough to mash with a fork, about 10 to 12 minutes. Drain the florets well and place into a bowl. Mash cauliflower and 1 tablespoon of milk with a fork, or use an immersion blender. Set aside.

Remove the lamb shanks from the pot and place on a plate. Mix together 2 teaspoons of arrowroot powder and 2 teaspoons of water until powder is dissolved, and add it to the pot to thicken the sauce.

To serve, divide mashed cauliflower on plates, and place lamb shanks on top of the cauliflower. Pour a generous amount of sauce on top.

Beer Braised Roast with Polenta

If you're looking for a filling and hearty dish, this is it! It's definitely suited for that favorite meat-and-potatoes person in your life, or if you simply want pure comfort food with a twist!

PREP TIME: 10 MINUTES

COOK TIME: 2 HOURS, 10 MINUTES

TOTAL TIME: 2 HOURS, 20 MINUTES

. . . .

Preheat oven to 300°F.

Season both sides of the chuck roast with salt and pepper.

In a large, oven-safe, heavy bottom pan, such as a Dutch oven, heat up vegetable oil over medium-high heat. Once the pan is hot, sear both sides of the chuck roast to brown. Remove the roast from the pan and set it on a plate. Remove the pan from heat.

Add the onion and carrots to the pan, and place the roast on top.

Cut the orange in half, and squeeze the juice into the pan. Place the juiced orange halves on either side of the roast. Sprinkle rosemary on top and pour beer over the roast.

Place in oven, covered, and cook for 2 hours and 10 minutes or until roast shreds easily when you poke it with a fork. Let roast rest for 20 minutes before you shred it.

When the roast is nearly done, cook polenta according to the directions on the package. Set aside.

Shred the roast with two forks and place back into the pot to soak up the juices.

To serve, spoon polenta onto the plates then place shredded roast, sauce, and vegetables on top.

1¼ pounds chuck roast

1½ teaspoons kosher salt

½ teaspoon ground black pepper

½ tablespoon vegetable oil

1 medium onion, sliced

2 carrots, cut into 1-inch long pieces

1 medium orange

½ tablespoon chopped rosemary

1 cup pale lager beer, such as Budweiser

¼ cup quick-cook polenta

. . . .

NOTE: Make sure you buy the right cut of meat. Chuck roast will yield unbelievably tender, shredded beef, but a different cut of meat could yield rock hard beef that is impossible to shred. If you are unsure about the cut of meat you're buying, check with your butcher.

Blackened Fish Tacos with Avocado Crema and Mango Cabbage Slaw

PREP TIME: 20 MINUTES
COOK TIME: 15 MINUTES
TOTAL TIME: 35 MINUTES

FOR THE SEASONING

1 tablespoon paprika

½ tablespoon each garlic powder and onion powder

½ teaspoon each dried oregano, dried basil, and dried thyme

Large pinch cayenne pepper

1 teaspoon kosher salt

FOR THE CABBAGE SLAW

2 cups diced mangos

1 cup finely shredded red cabbage

Juice of 1 lime

2 tablespoons chopped cilantro

FOR THE AVOCADO CREMA

½ avocado

2½ tablespoons sour cream

Juice of ½ lime

½ teaspoon kosher salt

2 teaspoons honey

FOR THE REMAINDER

2 tilapia fillets, about 1 pound total

2 tablespoons vegetable oil, divided

6 small corn tortillas, warmed

Taco Tuesday or Taco Thursday . . . whichever night you choose, this recipe will give your next taco night an oomph of flavor! You'll want to slather the avocado crema over every bite.

· ·

For the seasoning: In a small bowl, combine all the ingredients for the seasoning and stir to combine. Set aside.

For the cabbage slaw: In a medium bowl, toss the ingredients for the cabbage slaw together and set aside.

For the avocado crema: In the bowl of a food processor or the jar of a blender, add all the ingredients for the avocado crema, and process or blend until the mixture is smooth and no chunks remain.

For the remainder: Season both sides of the tilapia filets with the blackening seasoning.

In a large cast-iron skillet or nonstick skillet, over medium-high heat, heat 1 tablespoon of vegetable oil. Place one tilapia fillet into the pan and cook for 3 minutes on one side. Gently flip the tilapia fillet onto the other side and cook for another 3 minutes. Gently place fish onto a large plate and repeat with the remaining 1 tablespoon vegetable oil and tilapia fillet.

To assemble the fish tacos, using two forks, gently flake off chunks of the tilapia fillets. Place a bed of tilapia onto the bottom of a corn tortilla, add a generous amount of mango cabbage slaw, and drizzle the avocado crema on top.

Repeat for all the remaining tacos.

· ·

NOTE: Feel free to put a lot more avocado crema on top of the tacos. It gives the tacos great flavor!

Italian Sausage and Pepper Stromboli

My husband is half-Italian, and he knows what a good stromboli is like. Do you realize how much pressure I was under to perfect this recipe? Well, since you're reading this right now, my stromboli clearly passed the taste test!

PREP TIME: 25 MINUTES

COOK TIME: 45 MINUTES

TOTAL TIME: 1 HOUR, 10 MINUTES

. . . .

Bring store-bought or prepared dough to room temperature. In the meantime, cook the filling.

Add the vegetable oil to a medium skillet over medium-high heat. Sauté the onion, green bell pepper, and sausage. Using a wooden spoon, break up the sausage into smaller pieces. Cook until onions and green bell peppers are softened and sausage is cooked through, about 7 to 10 minutes. Set filling aside to cool.

Divide the dough into two equal pieces.

Preheat oven to 375°F.

On a lightly floured, flat surface, roll out one-half of the dough into a large circle. Add half the filling on one side of the dough. Sprinkle half the cheese on top of the filling. Pick up the other side of the dough and bring it over the filled side, pinching the edges together to seal. Carefully transfer to a baking sheet. Repeat with the second stromboli.

Brush the tops of the stromboli with the egg wash.

Place the baking sheet in the oven on the middle rack, and bake for 35 minutes or until stromboli is golden brown.

Cut in half, and serve with a side of marinara sauce.

. . . .

NOTE: Store-bought dough can differ in cooking time and baking temperature depending on the brand. Double-check the packaging for more information.

FOR THE DOUGH

1 package store-bought pizza dough or 1 recipe of your favorite homemade dough

FOR THE REMAINDER OF THIS DISH

½ tablespoon vegetable oil

½ medium onion, diced (about ¾ cup)

1 green bell pepper, diced (about ¾ cup)

2 fresh Italian sausages, casings removed

1 cup freshly grated mozzarella cheese

1 large egg, lightly beaten, for brushing

Marinara sauce, for dipping

Grilled Turkey Burgers with Arugula and Spicy Mayo

This is not just your regular turkey burger. If you've never had a moist and juicy turkey burger, your search is over! I had the most amazing turkey burger at a restaurant long ago and have been trying to re-create it for ages. I'm happy to say, I finally succeeded. Feel free to go overboard on the spicy mayo.

PREP TIME: 15 MINUTES
COOK TIME: 20 MINUTES
TOTAL TIME: 35 MINUTES

FOR THE SPICY MAYO

3 tablespoons mayo

1 teaspoon Sriracha sauce

FOR THE BURGERS

½ pound ground turkey

¼ cup diced red onion

2 teaspoons Worcestershire sauce

¼ teaspoon garlic powder

¼ cup Italian seasoned breadcrumbs

½ teaspoon kosher salt

½ teaspoon ground black pepper

1 large egg

⅓ cup shredded Colby jack cheese

1 tablespoon vegetable oil, divided

2 hamburger buns

2 cups loosely packed baby arugula leaves

For the mayo: In a small bowl, mix together the mayo and Sriracha sauce.

For the burgers: In a large bowl, gently mix together with your hands all the ingredients through Colby jack cheese until just combined. Don't overwork the meat.

Form two patties, about 1-inch thick.

In a medium skillet over medium-high heat, add ½ tablespoon of vegetable oil. Once oil has heated, add one turkey patty to the skillet. Brown both sides then turn heat down to medium and cook burger until internal temperature reaches 160°F, about 7 to 10 minutes. Remove the cooked turkey patty and place on a plate. Repeat with the other turkey patty.

To assemble the burgers, spread spicy mayo on both bottom and top buns, place a patty on one side of the bun and pile half the arugula on top. Put on the top bun. Repeat for the other burger.

Serve with a side of chips, salad, or french fries.

Eggplant Boats

f you're being health-conscious or just looking for a new way to stuff a vegetable, these eggplant boats are for you. They are fun and easy to make, and they let you present a meal in a different way. Cleanup is easy too!

PREP TIME: 30 MINUTES
COOK TIME: 35 MINUTES
TOTAL TIME: 1 HOUR,
5 MINUTES

Slice the eggplant in half, lengthwise, and scoop out the insides, being careful to leave a ¼-inch border around the sides and not to pierce the eggplant skin. Finely chop the meaty flesh of the eggplant and set it aside. Place the eggplant halves to the side.

Preheat oven to 375°F. Lightly grease a 9 × 13-inch, oven-safe casserole dish.

Heat olive oil in a large skillet over medium-high heat. Once the oil is hot, add the zucchini, onion, and garlic to the skillet. Sauté until softened, about 10 minutes. Add the mushrooms, eggplant flesh, and ground turkey to the skillet, crumbling the ground turkey with a spatula or wooden spoon. Continue to sauté until vegetables have softened and ground turkey has cooked through, about 5 to 7 minutes.

Add the tomato, oregano, basil, salt, and pepper. Toss to incorporate.

Remove skillet from heat and, using a large spoon, evenly divide the filling between the eggplant halves.

Evenly sprinkle mozzarella on top of the two eggplant halves, and gently place them into the prepared casserole dish.

Bake uncovered for 35 minutes. Let eggplants sit for 10 minutes prior to serving.

Directly serve eggplants onto plate.

- 1 large eggplant (about 1½ pounds)
- 1 tablespoon olive oil
- 1 large zucchini, diced (about 1 cup)
- ½ onion, diced (about ½ cup)
- 1 garlic clove, minced
- 5 ounces baby portobello mushrooms, finely chopped (about ½ cup)
- ½ pound ground turkey
- ¼ cup canned, diced tomatoes, drained
- ½ teaspoon dried oregano
- ½ teaspoon dried basil
- ½ teaspoon kosher salt
- ¼ teaspoon ground black pepper
- 1¼ cups freshly grated mozzarella cheese

Spicy Meatball Subs

PREP TIME: 20 MINUTES

COOK TIME: 10 MINUTES

TOTAL TIME: 30 MINUTES

¼ pound beef, pork, and veal mix (also known as meatloaf mix)

7 ounces hot Italian sausage, casings removed

1 large egg

¼ cup Italian seasoned breadcrumbs

½ teaspoon sweet paprika

½ teaspoon garlic powder

½ teaspoon kosher salt

Large pinch cayenne pepper

¼ teaspoon ground black pepper

1 tablespoon vegetable oil

2 (6-inch) sub rolls

Most meatball subs are awkward to eat. You end up getting sauce all over your face and hands while the person sitting across from you gives you *the look*. Let's just say that you should make these fiery subs at home where you and your dinner partner can give each other *the look* in private!

· ·

In a large bowl, combine beef, pork, and veal mix, Italian sausage, egg, breadcrumbs, and seasonings. Using your hands, gently mix ingredients together until just combined. Do not overwork the meat.

Form meat into 1-inch round meatballs. You should get 6 meatballs in the end.

In a large skillet over medium-high heat, add vegetable oil. Once the oil is hot, add the meatballs to the skillet, and brown all sides. Turn down the heat to medium-low, and cook the meatballs until cooked through or internal temperature reaches 160°F, about 10 minutes.

To assemble subs, place three meatballs on each sub roll, and add your favorite toppings. Some suggested toppings: mayo, pickles, tomatoes, and lettuce; even some marinara sauce would be great!

Chorizo and Sweet Potato Black Bean Chili

'm always trying to find new ways to make chili. It's one of those comfort foods that can be done up in classic style or can be given a twist. To me, chili is great year-round, because who doesn't need a hearty bowl of chili every now and then?

• •

In a large heavy-bottomed pot, like a Dutch oven, over medium-high heat, cook chorizo for 3 minutes and break it apart into crumbles with a wooden spoon or spatula. Add the onion, garlic, and green bell peppers. Sauté mixture together for 5 minutes.

Add the diced tomatoes, and then stir in the cumin, chili powder, salt, and black pepper. Stir to combine.

Add the sweet potato, kidney beans, black beans, and water. Stir well to combine all the ingredients.

Let mixture simmer covered for 15 minutes. Then remove the lid, and let simmer for 10 minutes more, or until the sweet potato is fork tender.

• •

NOTE: You can serve this chili with a multitude of toppings. Some ideas are sour cream, green onions, shredded cheese, and chopped avocado.

PREP TIME: 10 MINUTES
COOK TIME: 25 MINUTES
TOTAL TIME: 35 MINUTES

5 ounces fresh chorizo sausage, casing removed

1 medium onion, chopped (about 3/4 cup)

2 garlic cloves, minced

1 small green bell pepper, diced (about 1/2 cup)

1/2 cup canned, fire roasted, diced tomatoes, undrained

1/4 teaspoon ground cumin

1/4 teaspoon chili powder

1/2 teaspoon kosher salt

1/4 teaspoon ground black pepper

1 large sweet potato, cut into 1-inch cubes (about 2 cups), peeled and rinsed

3/4 cup canned, red kidney beans, drained and rinsed

1/2 cup canned, black beans, drained and rinsed

1 3/4 cups water

Broccoli Cheddar Soup

PREP TIME: 10 MINUTES

COOK TIME: 20 MINUTES

TOTAL TIME: 30 MINUTES

2 tablespoons unsalted butter

¾ cup shredded carrots

1 small onion, diced (about ½ cup)

1 garlic clove, minced

2 cups chicken broth

¼ cup heavy cream

2½ cups frozen broccoli florets

3 cups freshly grated, extra sharp, cheddar cheese

2 tablespoons all-purpose flour

1 teaspoon kosher salt, more to taste

½ teaspoon ground black pepper, more to taste

Broccoli cheddar soup is so easy to make at home that it makes me wonder why we always go out and buy it. By using a few simple ingredients, you can make yourself a classic soup right in your own home!

• •

In a large pot over medium-high heat, melt butter. Add shredded carrots, onion, and garlic to the pot. Cook until onion is slightly tender and translucent, about 5 minutes.

Turn the heat down to medium-low, and add the chicken broth and heavy cream. Stir, and let simmer for 5 minutes.

Add the broccoli florets and cheddar cheese. Stir until all the cheese has melted. Then sprinkle flour on top of the mixture, and whisk until incorporated. Add salt and pepper, then let simmer for 10 minutes or until mixture has thickened and cheese has completely melted through.

Serve in bread bowls or regular bowls with crusty bread.

Roasted Garlic and Potato Soup

This soup is packed full of flavor and is so easy to make. The velvety smooth texture is unbelievable!

. . . .

For the garlic: Preheat oven to 400°F.

Peel away the outer layers of the garlic bulbs, but leave the individual skins on the cloves intact.

Using a sharp knife, cut off the top ¼ to ½ inch of the garlic, exposing the individual cloves. Place the garlic heads on a sheet of foil, drizzle olive oil on top and sprinkle with a little salt. Then wrap it up, and place inside oven on the middle baking rack. Roast for 35 to 40 minutes. When the garlic is cool enough to touch, squeeze the entire garlic bulb over a small bowl. The softened cloves should squeeze right on out. Set aside.

For the remainder of the dish: While the garlic is roasting, bring a pot of water to a boil. Add the potatoes to the pot and reduce heat to medium-high. Cook until potatoes are softened and easily fall apart when pricked with a fork, about 20 minutes. After 15 minutes, add the onion to the pot to soften for about 5 minutes. Drain mixture and set aside.

In a blender or food processor, add chicken broth, heavy cream, roasted garlic, potatoes and onion, salt, and black pepper. If using a blender, remove the plastic piece in the lid, and place a towel on top to let steam escape.

Process mixture until smooth.

Serve warm with a side of bread or in a bread bowl, and sprinkle chives on top, if desired.

PREP TIME: 5 MINUTES
COOK TIME: 1 HOUR
TOTAL TIME: 1 HOUR,
5 MINUTES

FOR THE ROASTED GARLIC

1 head of garlic

Olive oil

Kosher salt

FOR THE REMAINDER OF DISH

3 medium potatoes (4 cups), peeled, rinsed, and cubed

½ small white onion, diced (about ½ cup)

2 cups chicken broth

1 tablespoon heavy cream

2 teaspoons kosher salt

½ teaspoon ground black pepper

Chives, for topping (optional)

Spicy Crab Bisque

PREP TIME: 5 MINUTES

COOK TIME: 20 MINUTES

TOTAL TIME: 25 MINUTES

2 teaspoons olive oil

1 shallot, finely chopped

1 garlic clove, minced

3 cups seafood broth

1 cup heavy cream

1½ tablespoons tomato paste

Large pinch cayenne pepper

1 teaspoon kosher salt

½ teaspoon ground black pepper

8 ounces lump crabmeat

1 tablespoon all-purpose flour

My husband and I have a favorite restaurant that serves the most velvety smooth crab bisque. I've always wanted to try to re-create it so that we don't have to spend a crazy amount of money for a small bowl. I love how easy this bisque was to make. We now make our favorite soup whenever we want, right in our own home!

· ·

In a large pot over medium-high heat, add olive oil. When oil is hot, add shallot and garlic, and sauté until fragrant, about 3 minutes. Reduce heat to medium. Then add the seafood broth, heavy cream, tomato paste, cayenne pepper, salt, and pepper. Whisk to break up the tomato paste.

Add the crabmeat to the mixture, and then whisk in the flour. Turn the heat down to medium-low, and let mixture simmer and thicken for 15 minutes.

Serve warm in bread bowls or in a large soup bowl with a side of crusty bread and side salad.

· ·

NOTE: If you like more heat, you can add more cayenne pepper to the soup.

Grilled Chicken and Kale Salad with Almond Honey Dijon Dressing

Sometimes, after a few days of eating not-so-healthy, my husband and I detox with a hearty salad for dinner. The dressing is, hands down, what makes this salad. You'll want to drizzle it over everything. A heavy pour is encouraged!

. . . .

For the dressing: In a bowl, whisk together all the dressing ingredients and set aside.

To assemble salad: Place all the salad ingredients in a large bowl. Toss to incorporate the ingredients evenly.

Drizzle salad dressing all over the salad then toss to coat well.

. . . .

NOTES: Some optional ingredients that you can consider for this salad: another favorite nut (such as walnuts or pecans), celery, sunflower seeds, or dried cranberries.

If you don't want to grill your chicken, you can cook it on the stovetop.

PREP TIME: 15 MINUTES
COOK TIME: 10 MINUTES
TOTAL TIME: 25 MINUTES

FOR THE DRESSING

¹/₂ cup almond butter

1 tablespoon + 1 teaspoon olive oil

1 tablespoon honey

2 teaspoons Dijon mustard (like Grey Poupon)

¹/₄ cup + 2 tablespoons water

2 teaspoons red wine vinegar

1 teaspoon kosher salt

FOR THE SALAD

2 grilled boneless, skinless chicken breasts, cut into cubes

4 cups loosely packed, finely chopped kale leaves

2 cups loosely packed, finely chopped radicchio

¹/₂ red onion, diced (about ¹/₂ cup)

²/₃ cup sliced almonds

Bacon and Shaved Brussels Sprouts Salad with Honey Lemon Vinaigrette

PREP TIME: 15 MINUTES

COOK TIME: N/A

TOTAL TIME: 15 MINUTES

FOR THE DRESSING

¼ cup olive oil

2 tablespoons champagne vinegar (or white wine vinegar or plain white vinegar)

4 tablespoons honey

Juice of 1 lemon

¼ teaspoon kosher salt

¼ teaspoon ground black pepper

1 teaspoon chia seeds (optional)

FOR THE SALAD

4 cups shredded Brussels sprouts

2 cups premade broccoli slaw

6 slices bacon, cooked crispy and roughly chopped

I f you aren't fond of Brussels sprouts, here's your chance to love them! Tossed together with a sweet and tangy honey lemon vinaigrette and lots of bacon, what's not to love?

· ·

For the dressing: In a small bowl, whisk together the dressing ingredients and set aside.

To assemble the salad: In a large bowl, toss together Brussels sprouts and broccoli slaw so everything is evenly distributed throughout. Add the chopped bacon, and then drizzle with dressing. Toss again to incorporate.

You can serve this room temperature, or you can pop this in the refrigerator for 1 to 2 hours and serve it chilled.

· ·

NOTE: We like to serve this salad with a side of crusty bread.

BREAKFAST for DINNER

Fluffy Buttermilk Pancakes with Blueberry Compote

We love a fluffy buttermilk pancake—none of that rubbery box-mixed kind! This pancake recipe yields the fluffiest and lightest pancakes we've ever eaten. Best of all, you can use this recipe over and over again for any pancake variation you want.

. . . .

For the blueberry compote: In a small pot, over medium heat, combine the compote ingredients and let simmer until blueberries are softened and burst and the mixture has thickened, about 15 minutes. Set aside.

For the pancakes: In a large bowl, whisk together flour, baking powder, baking soda, salt, and sugar. Make a well in the center of the mixture, and add the egg and buttermilk. Whisk the batter well (see note) until no lumps remain and the ingredients are all incorporated.

Spray a large skillet or griddle with cooking spray and place over medium heat.

Using a 1/3 measuring cup, drop batter into the skillet or griddle. When bubbles start to form on top of the batter, it is ready to flip. Each side should take about 2 minutes.

Repeat until all the batter has been used up. You should get about 5 or 6 pancakes.

Serve pancakes with blueberry compote on top.

. . . .

NOTE: This pancake batter has the thick consistency of a cake batter. That's how it's supposed to be. You can certainly thin it out to yield more pancakes. If you do thin out the batter and end up with more pancakes than you can eat, don't worry—you can freeze them for another time!

PREP TIME: 10 MINUTES
COOK TIME: 25 MINUTES
TOTAL TIME: 35 MINUTES

FOR THE BLUEBERRY COMPOTE

2 cups frozen blueberries

2 teaspoons lemon juice

1/4 cup granulated sugar

1 1/2 teaspoons water

FOR THE PANCAKES

1 1/2 cups all-purpose flour

1 1/2 teaspoons baking powder

3/4 teaspoon baking soda

1/2 teaspoon kosher salt

2 tablespoons granulated sugar

1 large egg

3/4 cup buttermilk

Banana Pecan Bourbon Flapjacks

PREP TIME: 10 MINUTES

COOK TIME: 25 MINUTES

TOTAL TIME: 35 MINUTES

FOR THE BANANA PECAN BOURBON TOPPING

2 bananas, sliced into rounds

1/3 cup maple syrup

1 tablespoon bourbon whiskey

1/2 cup roughly chopped pecans

FOR THE PANCAKES

1 1/2 cups all-purpose flour

1 1/2 teaspoons baking powder

3/4 teaspoon baking soda

1/2 teaspoon kosher salt

2 tablespoons granulated sugar

1 large egg

3/4 cup buttermilk

The title of this recipe might just make you want to immediately get in your kitchen and whip up dinner. These are the same fluffy buttermilk pancakes described in the preceding recipe, but the banana pecan bourbon topping here is seriously awesome. You'll wonder how you've gone without it for so long in your life.

· ·

For the topping: In a small skillet over medium heat, add the topping ingredients. Let simmer and thicken for 10 minutes, stirring occasionally to prevent burning. Set aside.

For the pancakes: In a large bowl, whisk together flour, baking powder, baking soda, salt, and sugar. Make a well in the center of the mixture and add the egg and buttermilk. Whisk the batter well (see note) until no lumps remain and the batter is all incorporated.

Spray a large skillet or griddle with cooking spray and place over medium heat.

Using a 1/3 measuring cup, drop batter into the skillet or griddle. When bubbles start to form on top of the batter, it is ready to flip. Each side should take about 2 minutes each.

Repeat until all the batter has been used up. You should get 5 or 6 pancakes.

Serve pancakes with banana pecan bourbon topping and additional maple syrup, if desired.

· ·

NOTE: This pancake batter has the thick consistency of a cake batter. That's how it's supposed to be. You can certainly thin it out to yield more pancakes. If you do thin out the batter and end up with more pancakes than you can eat, don't worry—you can freeze them for another time!

Oven-Fried Chicken with Waffles and White Gravy

Fried chicken and waffles is such a classic brunch. This recipe takes the frying out of the chicken, 'cause who really wants to deal with that after a long day? I personally think the crust on this chicken is way better than the traditional fried crust. Anyway, you're going to love this version of "fried" chicken and waffles!

• •

Preheat oven to 400°F, and line a baking sheet with parchment paper or a silicone baking mat.

For the chicken: On a cutting board or flat surface, rub the chicken breast halves with mayonnaise, and then generously coat all sides of the chicken with the crushed potato chips. It's okay if they don't all stick to it.

Carefully place chicken onto prepared baking sheet, and bake on the middle rack in the oven for 15 to 17 minutes or until chicken is cooked through and outer crust is slightly browned. Once done, remove from oven and set on a plate inside the microwave to keep warm, or place into a warming drawer.

For the waffles: While the chicken is baking, preheat waffle maker.

In a small bowl, using a hand mixer, beat egg white and 1 tablespoon sugar until light and fluffy and forming soft peaks. Set aside.

In a large bowl, whisk flour, the remaining 1 tablespoon sugar, baking powder, baking soda, and salt. Make a well in the center of the batter, and pour in melted butter and buttermilk. Whisk until mixture is combined and no lumps remain. Using a spatula, gently fold in the egg whites. Be careful to mix until just incorporated. Do not overmix.

Using a ¾ cup measuring cup (see notes), scoop batter, and pour onto heated waffle iron. Cook until waffle is browned and

PREP TIME: 30 MINUTES
COOK TIME: 35 MINUTES
TOTAL TIME: 1 HOUR,
5 MINUTES

FOR THE OVEN-FRIED CHICKEN

1 large boneless, skinless, chicken breast, sliced in half lengthwise

3 tablespoons mayonnaise

1 cup finely crushed salt and pepper kettle-cooked potato chips

FOR THE WAFFLES

1 large egg white

2 tablespoons granulated sugar, divided

1¼ cups all-purpose flour

1½ teaspoons baking powder

¼ teaspoon baking soda

¼ teaspoon kosher salt

2 tablespoons unsalted butter, melted

¾ cup + 2 tablespoons buttermilk

(continued on page 126)

(continued from page 125)

**FOR THE WHITE
PEPPER GRAVY**

2 tablespoons unsalted
butter

2 tablespoons all-
purpose flour

1/2 cup + 2 teaspoons milk

1/4 teaspoon kosher salt

1/4 teaspoon ground
black pepper

crispy on the outside, about 5 minutes. Repeat for the second waffle. Once the waffles are done, place inside microwave or in a warming drawer.

For the gravy: In a small pot over medium heat, melt butter and whisk together with flour for about 2 minutes. Add the milk, salt, and pepper. Let simmer and thicken for about 5 minutes. Remove from heat.

To assemble waffle dish, place waffle on a plate and place the chicken on top. Then generously pour gravy on top of chicken and waffles. Repeat for the second waffle dish.

Serve warm, and enjoy.

• •

NOTES: These waffles take the additional step of forming soft fluffy peaks with the egg whites, but it is so worth it. It makes the waffles light and airy with a crispy outside. Don't skip this step!

The amount of waffle batter you measure will depend on what type of waffle maker you're using. I use a Belgian waffle maker. To make sure you don't overflow the waffle maker, start with a smaller amount of batter and then build up.

Leek Apple Sausage Baked French Toast

Salty with a hint of sweetness is what you'll get in this breakfast (for dinner) bake! It reminds me of a crisp fall day. I love prepping this dish before work in the morning and then popping it in the oven when I get home.

PREP TIME: 15 MINUTES
COOK TIME: 1 HOUR
TOTAL TIME: 1 HOUR, 15 MINUTES

- 6 ounces breakfast sausage
- 2 cups chopped leeks
- 1½ cups diced Granny Smith apples (approximately 1 apple)
- ¼ teaspoon kosher salt
- 4 cups 2-inch cubed challah bread
- 3 large eggs
- 1½ cups milk

· ·

Preheat oven to 375°F, and lightly grease a 2-quart casserole dish.

In a large skillet over medium high heat, brown the sausage and break it up with a wooden spoon or spatula. Once the sausage has cooked through, about 5 minutes, add the leeks and apples. Cook until leeks are slightly softened, about 3–5 minutes. The apples will finish cooking in the oven. Season with salt. Toss until everything is thoroughly incorporated.

Cover the bottom of your prepared casserole dish with a layer of challah bread. Add all the sausage mixture on top, followed by the remaining challah bread. You'll need to use the back of your wooden spoon or spatula to press down the bread and squish it all in.

In a measuring cup, whisk together eggs and milk.

Gently pour all over the bread mixture, pressing it down as you pour the egg and milk mixture on top.

Cover tightly with foil and place on a baking sheet in case it spills over. Place baking sheet on the middle rack in the oven and bake for 60 minutes. In the last 15 minutes of baking, remove foil.

Let rest for 10 minutes, and then cut and serve.

· ·

NOTE: You can cover this dish, let it sit in the refrigerator overnight, and then bake it the next day if you prefer.

Ham and Gruyère Stuffed French Toast

PREP TIME: 15 MINUTES
COOK TIME: 30 MINUTES
TOTAL TIME: 45 MINUTES

½ cup milk

2 large eggs

4 large slices bread, cut 2-inch thick

4 slices thick-cut ham (or deli ham)

1½ cups freshly grated Gruyère cheese, plus more for topping, if desired

2 tablespoons unsalted butter, divided

Stuffed French toast is such a great invention. I mean, regular French toast is already great in and of itself, but stuffing it with gooey cheese and meat just takes it to a whole other level—a level that you want to be on. Your taste buds will be thanking you!

. . . .

Preheat oven to 375°F, and line a baking sheet with parchment paper or silicone baking mat.

In a shallow container, whisk together milk and eggs. Set aside.

Place the 4 slices of bread on a flat surface. With a small serrated knife, cut halfway down in the middle of each slice, like butterflying the bread, but be careful not to slice all the way through; otherwise you won't be able to stuff it. Repeat for each slice.

Gently fill the center of each bread slice with ¼ of the ham and cheese. Close them tightly then dip both sides of each slice into the milk and egg mixture.

Heat up a medium skillet over medium heat, and melt 1½ teaspoons butter.

Carefully place one of the coated slices into the skillet and brown on both sides. Place bread onto prepared baking sheet.

Repeat until all slices have been browned on both sides.

Sprinkle more cheese on top, if desired.

Place baking sheet on the middle rack in the oven, and bake for 25 to 30 minutes or until cheese is melted and sandwich is warmed through.

Remove from oven and serve.

Roasted Poblano and Chorizo Strata

I love coming home from work knowing that dinner is already prepped and ready for me to pop in the oven. This is another one of those prep-ahead dishes that's so good it'll have you jetting out of your workplace as soon as it hits five o'clock!

· ·

Preheat oven to 375°F and lightly grease a 2-quart casserole dish.

To roast the poblano peppers, turn the flame on your gas stove-top on high, and place the poblano peppers onto the grates. (Don't have a gas stove? You can do this on a grill or under a broiler.) Using tongs, flip the poblano peppers about every 20 to 30 seconds. Char just their skin sides, being careful not to burn them. Afterward, place them in a bowl, seal it well with plastic wrap, and let the steam do its job. After about 30 minutes, peel the skin off the outside.

In a large skillet over medium-high heat, brown the chorizo and break it up with your wooden spoon. Add chopped poblano peppers and toss to incorporate.

Cover the bottom of prepared casserole dish with a layer of challah bread. Add all the chorizo filling on top, sprinkle on the Cotija cheese, and then top with the remaining challah bread. You'll need to use the back of a wooden spoon or spatula to press down the bread and squish it all in.

In a measuring cup, whisk together eggs and milk. Gently pour all over the bread mixture, pressing down as you pour the egg and milk mixture on top. Cover tightly with foil and place on a baking sheet. Bake for 60 minutes on the middle rack in the oven. In the last 15 minutes of baking, remove foil.

Let rest for 10 minutes, then cut and serve.

· ·

NOTES: You can cover the dish with foil, place it in the refrigerator overnight, and then bake the next morning.

PREP TIME: 30 MINUTES
COOK TIME: 1 HOUR
TOTAL TIME: 1 HOUR,
30 MINUTES

2 large poblano peppers, roasted, deseeded, and chopped

¾ pound fresh chorizo sausage, casings removed

4 cups 2-inch cubed challah bread

1 cup Cotija cheese or crumbled feta cheese

3 large eggs

1½ cups milk

Smoked Sausage and Spinach Tater Tot Breakfast Bake

PREP TIME: 10 MINUTES

COOK TIME: 60 MINUTES

TOTAL TIME: 1 HOUR, 10 MINUTES

6 ounces smoked sausage, sliced into rounds and quartered

4 cups loosely packed baby spinach leaves

4 large eggs

2/3 cup milk

1 cup freshly grated cheddar cheese, divided

1/2 teaspoon kosher salt

1/4 teaspoon ground black pepper

25–30 frozen tater tots

Sriracha or hot sauce, for topping (optional)

f I could eat tater tots every day, I'd be one happy girl. I went over the top with this baked egg dish by topping it off with tater tots. We couldn't stop eating it—the tater tot "crust" is probably one of the best things ever!

· ·

Preheat oven to 400°F, and lightly grease an oven-safe, 1-quart casserole dish.

In a large skillet over medium-high heat, brown sausage on both sides, about 5 to 7 minutes. Add the spinach and sauté until wilted. Remove from heat.

In a large bowl, whisk together eggs, milk, 1/2 cup cheddar cheese, salt, and pepper.

Add the sausage and spinach to the bowl with the egg mixture, and then pour into the prepared casserole dish.

Carefully place the tater tots on top of the egg mixture. It's okay if some of them sink. Sprinkle remaining 1/2 cup of cheese on top of tater tots.

Carefully place the casserole dish onto a baking sheet, in case it spills over while baking. Place on the middle rack in the oven, and bake for 60 minutes uncovered or until the egg is completely set.

Let cool for 10 minutes before slicing and serving.

Drizzle with Sriracha sauce or hot sauce, if desired.

Breakfast Enchilada Gratin

Let's be honest, enchiladas are super delicious but rolling up each one individually and perfectly is a chore. This casserole has all the flavors of an enchilada, plus a ridiculously awesome potato topping. It's so delicious you won't miss those perfectly rolled tortillas!

. . . .

Preheat oven to 400°F, and lightly grease a 1-quart, oven-safe casserole dish.

Slice the potato into ⅛-inch discs with a sharp knife or mandolin slicer. Place the potato discs into a bowl and cover with cold water to prevent browning. Set aside.

In a medium bowl, whisk together eggs, milk, spices, corn kernels, black beans, diced green chilies, salt, and pepper.

Pour egg mixture into prepared casserole dish place into oven on the middle rack, and bake for 20 minutes uncovered.

In the meantime, dry potato discs with paper towels. Once the egg mixture has baked for 20 minutes, carefully remove from the oven, and place potato discs on top of the egg mixture. It's okay if they overlap and if some sink into the egg mixture.

Sprinkle cheese on top of the potatoes, and bake for another 30 minutes uncovered until potato slices are cooked through and softened.

Cut into wedges and serve.

PREP TIME: 15 MINUTES

COOK TIME: 50 MINUTES

TOTAL TIME: 1 HOUR, 5 MINUTES

1 large russet potato (about ¾ pound), peeled and rinsed

4 large eggs

¼ cup milk

2 teaspoons ground chili powder

¼ teaspoon garlic powder

½ teaspoon ground cumin

¼ teaspoon ground sweet paprika

¼ teaspoon ground cayenne

½ cup frozen corn kernels

½ cup canned black beans, drained and rinsed

1 (10-ounce) can diced, green chilies, drained

1 teaspoon kosher salt

¼ teaspoon ground black pepper

¾ cup freshly grated, sharp cheddar cheese

Chorizo, Kale, and Sun-Dried Tomato Frittata

PREP TIME: 15 MINUTES

COOK TIME: 30 MINUTES

TOTAL TIME: 45 MINUTES

10 ounces fresh chorizo sausage, casings removed

4 cups chopped kale, loosely packed

¼ cup sun-dried tomato halves

4 large eggs

¼ cup half-and-half

¾ cup milk

½ teaspoon kosher salt

¼ teaspoon ground black pepper

Frittatas are one of my favorite breakfast-for-dinner items to make because of their versatility. This recipe calls for three of my favorite frittata ingredients, and the results are fantastic and so filling!

. . . .

Preheat oven to 350°F, and lightly grease a 10-inch round, oven-safe skillet or cast-iron skillet.

In a separate large skillet, brown chorizo sausage over medium-high heat and break it apart into pieces with your spatula or wooden spoon. Once the chorizo is almost done, about 7 minutes, add the kale and sun-dried tomatoes. Toss to incorporate. Remove from heat when kale has reduced down, about 5 minutes.

In a medium bowl, whisk together eggs, half-and-half, milk, salt, and pepper.

Pour the chorizo mixture into the prepared skillet, and then pour the egg mixture evenly over the chorizo mixture.

Place uncovered skillet on the middle rack in the oven, and bake for 30 minutes or until egg mixture has cooked completely through and no longer jiggles in the center.

Cut into wedges and serve.

Cheddar, Bacon, and Jalapeño Frittata

Cheddar, bacon, and jalapeño is a classic combination that just works. This frittata looks big, circumference-wise, but it's really thin, so there's not a lot of volume. I bet you'll eat it all in one sitting!

. . . .

Preheat oven to 350°F, and lightly grease a 10-inch round, oven-safe skillet or cast-iron skillet.

In a large bowl, whisk together all the ingredients.

Pour egg mixture into the prepared pan.

Place uncovered skillet on the middle rack of the oven, and bake for 30 minutes or until egg mixture has cooked completely through and no longer jiggles in the center.

Cut into wedges and serve.

PREP TIME: 5 MINUTES
COOK TIME: 30 MINUTES
TOTAL TIME: 35 MINUTES

4 large eggs

¼ cup half-and-half

¾ cup milk

1 jalapeño, deseeded and diced

1 cup freshly grated, cheddar cheese

6 slices bacon, cooked and chopped into pieces

Deconstructed Sausage, Egg, and Cheese Biscuit

PREP TIME: 15 MINUTES

COOK TIME: 20 MINUTES

TOTAL TIME: 35 MINUTES

FOR THE BISCUITS

1 cup all-purpose flour

1¹⁄₂ teaspoons baking powder

¹⁄₄ teaspoon kosher salt

3 tablespoons cold, unsalted butter, cut into cubes

¹⁄₂ cup milk

FOR THE REMAINDER OF THE DISH

¹⁄₂ pound breakfast sausage

2 large eggs

¹⁄₂ cup freshly grated cheddar cheese

Ah, the classic sausage, egg, and cheese biscuit. It's practically a staple for us on weekend mornings, but sometimes we make it for dinner! This is where this deconstructed sandwich comes into play—it provides a larger portion for dinner but still gives the same breakfast effect.

. . . .

For the biscuits: Preheat the oven to 425°F, and line a baking sheet with parchment paper or a silicone baking mat.

In a medium bowl, whisk together flour, baking powder, and salt. Using a pastry blender or two forks, cut the butter into the flour until it resembles pea-sized crumbles. Pour in the milk and stir until everything is mixed together and combined. The dough will be really sticky.

Gently flour your hands then divide the dough into equal halves. Form a ball with the dough, place it on the baking sheet, and then pat it down gently so it's about ²⁄₃-inch in height. Do the same with the other half of the dough.

Place baking sheet on the middle rack in the oven and bake for 12 minutes.

While biscuits are baking, brown the breakfast sausage in a small skillet, using a wooden spoon or spatula to break it apart. Set aside in a bowl.

Cook the eggs however you like: scrambled, fried, over easy, etc.

To assemble, place one biscuit on a plate. Use a fork to break it into smaller pieces, but keep them in bigger chunks. Sprinkle half the sausage mixture on top, then the cheese, and finally the egg on top. Repeat with the second biscuit and remaining ingredients.

Corned Beef Hash Eggs Benedict

For as long as I can remember, I have always loved corned beef. Reuben sandwiches were my favorite while growing up. I love the idea of corned beef and potatoes topped with a poached egg. It's a hearty dish that will keep you satisfied!

PREP TIME: 10 MINUTES

COOK TIME: 20 MINUTES

TOTAL TIME: 30 MINUTES

½ tablespoon vegetable oil

2 cups diced potatoes

1 cup chopped corned beef

½ teaspoon kosher salt

¼ teaspoon ground black pepper

2 poached eggs (see note)

Parsley for garnish (optional)

· ·

Heat the vegetable oil, using a large skillet over medium-high heat. Add the potatoes and shake the skillet to get the potatoes in an even layer. Cook until browned on all sides and softened through, 15 to 20 minutes.

Add the corned beef, and toss to incorporate. Season with salt and pepper.

To assemble, divide corned beef and potato mixture onto plates and gently place poached egg on top. Garnish with parsley, if using. Serve with cornbread, if desired.

· ·

NOTE: To poach eggs, bring a small pot of water to a boil, then lower the heat to medium. Add 1 teaspoon of plain vinegar to the pot, and stir to incorporate. The vinegar helps keep the egg whites from spreading out.

Crack a fresh egg into a ramekin. Using a wooden spoon, gently stir the water in a circular motion until the water creates a funnel-like shape in the center of the water. Carefully pour the egg into the center of the pot and use the wooden spoon to push some of the egg whites closer to the egg yolk. Cook the egg for 3 to 4 minutes. The egg whites should be completely cooked, and the egg yolks will still be runny. Please note that the timing will depend entirely on the size of your eggs. If you find that the yolk is too cooked for your liking, reduce cooking time for the next egg.

Remove the egg from the water with a slotted spoon and gently place it on a plate while you poach the other egg. Season both eggs with salt and pepper to taste.

Garden Vegetable Egg Bake

This egg bake doesn't look like much, but it packs a ton of flavor. Plus the servings are so cute in their little baking dishes. My husband became enamored with this dish. After every bite, he tells me how amazing it is and how perfect the flavors are. If that sort of response isn't enough to get you to make this, I'm not sure what else would! Did I mention how cute these look?

PREP TIME: 15 MINUTES
COOK TIME: 35 MINUTES
TOTAL TIME: 50 MINUTES

1 tablespoon olive oil

1 small onion, diced (about ½ cup)

½ yellow squash, diced (about 1 cup)

1 small red pepper, diced (about ⅔ cup)

4 ounces baby portobello mushrooms, thinly sliced

3 cups loosely packed baby spinach leaves

¾ cup medium chunky salsa (mild or spicy, if preferred)

½ cup crumbled feta cheese

2 large eggs

Preheat oven to 400°F, and lightly grease two oven-safe, 12-ounce soup crock bowls or similar.

Heat olive oil in a large skillet over medium-high heat, and then add onions, squash, and red peppers to the skillet. Cook until they're tender, about 7 minutes.

Add the mushrooms and spinach to the skillet. Cook until mushrooms have softened and spinach has wilted down, about 5 to 7 minutes. Remove from heat.

To assemble the bowls: In the bottom of each crock bowl, add a thin layer of chunky salsa. Then, layer on ¼ of the vegetable mixture. Next, layer ¼ cup feta cheese, then another layer of salsa, and, finally, layer on another ¼ of the vegetable mixture into each crock bowl.

Using a butter knife or your fingers, make a well in the center of the vegetable mixture, and crack an egg in each well.

Place in the oven on the middle rack, uncovered, for 20 minutes or just until the egg is cooked but still a bit runny.

Prior to serving, break the egg, and toss everything around to incorporate.

Serve and enjoy.

Tex-Mex Migas

This is an easy Southwestern Tex-Mex–style breakfast dish that is great for dinner. It'll satiate that Tex-Mex craving you may have. I love the added crunch and saltiness of the tortilla chips throughout the dish so much that I sometimes add more on top while eating it. Try it—you can't go wrong!

PREP TIME: 10 MINUTES
COOK TIME: 12 MINUTES
TOTAL TIME: 22 MINUTES

½ tablespoon vegetable oil

2 cups chopped bell peppers

½ cup diced onions

1 (15-ounce) can diced tomatoes, drained

6 large eggs

2 cups crushed tortilla chips

½ teaspoon kosher salt

¼ teaspoon ground black pepper

Cilantro, for garnish (optional)

· ·

Add vegetable oil to a medium skillet over medium-high heat and add the bell peppers and onion. Cook until softened, about 5 minutes. Add the diced tomatoes and eggs. Scramble everything together, and cook for 5 to 7 minutes or until eggs are cooked through.

Add the tortilla chips on top, toss gently to incorporate, and season with salt and pepper.

Garnish with cilantro, if using.

Smoked Salmon Eggs Benedict with Chipotle Hollandaise

PREP TIME: 10 MINUTES
COOK TIME: 10 MINUTES
TOTAL TIME: 20 MINUTES

FOR THE CHIPOTLE HOLLANDAISE SAUCE

8 tablespoons unsalted butter, melted

3 large eggs

1 teaspoon lemon juice

1/4–1/2 teaspoon chipotle powder

Water, if needed to thin out hollandaise

FOR THE REST OF THE DISH

1 avocado, sliced in half and pit removed

1/2 teaspoon kosher salt

1/4 teaspoon ground black pepper

2 English muffins, sliced in half

5 ounces thinly sliced smoked salmon

2 large eggs, poached

Eggs Benedict is such a classic breakfast dish that is easy to jazz up with smoked salmon. Dishes like this make the concept of dinner for breakfast easy to embrace. We love having breakfast for dinner, because most mornings we jet out the door and don't have time for a proper sit-down breakfast. So we have it in the evening instead!

· ·

For the hollandaise sauce: In a small skillet, melt butter over medium heat. Set aside to cool just slightly, about 2 minutes.

In the jar of your blender, pulse together the eggs, lemon juice, and chipotle powder.

With the blender on high, drizzle melted butter through the top of the blender and blend until mixture has thickened. If it's too thick, use water to thin it out. Set aside.

For the remainder of the dish: Using a metal spoon, scoop out the avocado flesh and put it into a small bowl. With the back of a fork, smash the avocado until no big chunks remain. Season with salt and pepper.

To assemble dish: Using a knife, spread smashed avocado evenly on the bottom and top halves of the English muffin. Top with slices of smoked salmon, then gently place poached egg on top. Generously top with chipotle hollandaise.

Repeat with the other English muffin and serve.

· ·

NOTE: See Corned Beef Hash Eggs Benedict recipe (page 145) for tips on poaching eggs.

Pancetta and Spinach Crêpes

Sweet crêpes are fantastic, but I wanted to do something different and make savory crêpes. These crêpes are just as simple to make as the sweet ones, but you can actually eat these for dinner without feeling too guilty!

. . . .

For the crêpes: In a medium bowl, whisk together the crêpes ingredients, then pour into a measuring cup for easy pouring into the pan.

Heat the 2 tablespoons butter in a small nonstick skillet over medium heat. Pour about ¼ cup of the crêpes batter into the skillet. As soon as you add the batter to the skillet, start gently turning the pan in circles to spread out the batter. Let sit for 2 minutes, then it should be ready to flip. To tell if it's ready to flip: using tongs, gently lift up on the crêpe edge and take a peek at the bottom to see that it is slightly browned and solid with no liquid left. If there is still a little liquid left, let it cook for another 30 seconds and then flip. Cook the other side for 2 minutes, and place the cooked crêpe on a plate. Repeat with the remaining batter. The batter will make between 8 and 10 crêpes, depending on how big you make them. They should be very thin, but they can be bigger in diameter depending on your skillet size.

Prepare the filling: Once you are finished making the crêpes, melt the 1 tablespoon butter in the same skillet. Cook pancetta and spinach until spinach has wilted and pancetta is warmed through.

To assemble: Place 4 or 5 crêpes on a plate, folded into quarter-shaped wedges, and top with half the pancetta and spinach mixture. Repeat with the remaining crêpes and pancetta and spinach mixture.

PREP TIME: 10 MINUTES
COOK TIME: 30 MINUTES
TOTAL TIME: 40 MINUTES

FOR THE CRÊPES

1 cup all-purpose flour

½ cup milk

½ cup water

2 large eggs

2 tablespoons unsalted butter

FOR THE FILLING

1 tablespoon unsalted butter

4 ounces diced pancetta

2 cups baby spinach

Hash Brown Waffle Huevos Rancheros

PREP TIME: 10 MINUTES
COOK TIME: 20 MINUTES
TOTAL TIME: 30 MINUTES

FOR THE HASH BROWN WAFFLES

3 cups frozen shredded potatoes, divided

2 large eggs

1 teaspoon kosher salt, divided

½ teaspoon ground black pepper, divided

FOR THE TOPPING

½ cup medium chunky salsa (mild or spicy, if preferred)

1 avocado, sliced, for topping

2 fried eggs

Have you ever thought to use your waffle maker to make hash brown waffles? I never imagined this was a possibility until I gave it a try. I honestly can't stop making hash brown waffles now. It's a really fun way to have shredded potatoes for breakfast or dinner!

· ·

For the waffle: Preheat waffle maker on high.

In a large bowl, mix together 1½ cups frozen shredded potatoes, 1 egg, ½ teaspoon salt, and ¼ teaspoon pepper.

Place mixture onto heated waffle maker, and cook for 7 to 10 minutes until golden brown.

Repeat with the remaining ingredients.

Assemble the dish: Once the waffles are done, place on plates, and top each waffle with salsa, avocado, and a fried egg.

Serve and enjoy.

Loaded Taco Tots

My love for tater tots won't ever die. I could eat them for every meal. This loaded tater tot dish is an awesome alternative to loaded nachos. After you make your first batch, I bet you won't be able to stop thinking about them. We can hardly contain ourselves when these come out of the oven!

· ·

Bake the tater tots according to the directions on the package. Once done, remove from oven and turn the oven to 350°F. Have an oven-safe, 9-inch diameter pie dish on hand.

In a medium skillet over medium-high heat, brown ground beef and break it up into smaller pieces with your spatula or wooden spoon. Cook until ground beef is cooked through, about 5 to 7 minutes. Add the onion, chili powder, cumin, and garlic powder. Cook until onion is softened, about 4 minutes.

Stir in the black beans and tomatoes. Stir to incorporate everything. Remove from heat.

Spread 2/3 of the ground beef mixture into the bottom of the pie dish. Add the tater tots on top, and then sprinkle the remainder of the ground beef mixture over the tater tots.

Sprinkle cheddar cheese on top and add the jalapeño slices, if using.

Bake uncovered for 15 minutes, or until cheese is melted.

Serve warm.

PREP TIME: 15 MINUTES
COOK TIME: 25 MINUTES
TOTAL TIME: 40 MINUTES

25 tater tots (about 2 cups)

1/2 pound ground beef

1 small onion, diced (about 1/2 cup)

2 teaspoons chili powder

1/2 teaspoon ground cumin

1/4 teaspoon garlic powder

1/2 cup canned black beans, drained and rinsed

1 (10-ounce) can tomatoes with cilantro and jalapeños (or tomatoes with green chilies), drained

2/3 cup freshly grated, cheddar cheese

10 jalapeño slices (optional)

Cowboy Skillet Hash

PREP TIME: 10 MINUTES
COOK TIME: 30 MINUTES
TOTAL TIME: 40 MINUTES

½ pound chorizo
    sausage, casings
    removed

1 small onion, diced
    (about ½ cup)

1 cup diced bell
    peppers of various
    colors

2 potatoes, diced into
    cubes (about 2 cups)

1 teaspoon kosher salt

¼ teaspoon ground
    black pepper

I love the name of this dish. It reminds me of a stick-to-your-ribs dish that someone on a ranch would want to eat after a day of herding cattle. It's okay, though; if you don't herd cattle during your work day, you're still more than welcome to eat this skillet dinner!

• •

In a large skillet over medium-high heat, brown the chorizo sausage, breaking it up with a wooden spoon or spatula as it cooks.

Once the chorizo has mostly cooked through; about 5 to 7 minutes, add the onion and bell peppers. Cook until onion and bell peppers have softened, about 7 to 10 minutes.

Add the potatoes to the skillet and sprinkle in the salt and pepper.

Continue cooking the hash over medium-high heat, stirring often, for about 20 minutes or until the potatoes have softened and cooked through.

Serve warm.

Shakshuka Breakfast Pizza

Shakshuka is a traditional Mediterranean dish that consists of poached eggs in a sauce of tomatoes, chili peppers, and onion. The dish is most often seasoned with cumin and sweet paprika. This is a super comforting breakfast dish, and it's even more fun in pizza form for dinner!

. . . .

Preheat oven to 400°F, and line two baking sheets with parchment paper or silicone baking mats.

For the sauce: Add olive oil to a small pot over medium-high heat. Sauté the onion, bell pepper, cherry peppers, and garlic until softened, about 10 minutes.

Carefully add the can of tomatoes, and then add paprika, cumin, and tomato paste. Stir to incorporate and let simmer for 20 minutes, stirring often.

At the end of the 20 minutes, add the crumbled feta cheese and stir to incorporate. Remove from heat.

To assemble: Place two pitas onto each prepared baking sheet. Divide and spread the shakshuka sauce mixture evenly amongst the pitas.

Make a small well in the center of the sauce, and carefully crack an egg into it. It's okay if it spills off the side.

Carefully place baking sheets into the oven on the middle rack. Bake for 25 to 30 minutes or until egg is just cooked and still a bit runny.

Slice into wedges and serve.

PREP TIME: 10 MINUTES
COOK TIME: 1 HOUR
TOTAL TIME: 1 HOUR,
10 MINUTES

**FOR THE
SHAKSHUKA SAUCE**

½ tablespoon olive oil

1 medium onion, diced
(about ¾ cup)

1 small yellow bell
pepper, sliced into
thin strips

4 small cherry peppers,
quartered

1 garlic clove, minced

1 (14.5-ounce) can, fire
roasted tomatoes,
undrained

1 teaspoon sweet
paprika

1 teaspoon ground
cumin

½ tablespoon tomato
paste

½ cup crumbled feta
cheese

**FOR THE REST
OF THE PIZZA**

4 large pitas, about
7 inches in diameter

4 large eggs

Acknowledgments

TO ALL MY FRIENDS AND FAMILY—I know it hasn't been an easy year with me never being able to hang out or catch up, but I want you to know that I appreciate the understanding and continued support. You guys are the best. Thank you!

TO MY RECIPE TESTERS—Lindsey Allan, Sarah Alvarez, Sarah and Adam Fingerman, Jessica Fols, Kristell Fonseca, Casey and Justin Gallamore, Andrea Greenwich, Amanda Jones, Pamela Kennedy, Allison Neal, Patti Pfeiff, Megan Piferi, and Lisa Wampler. Thank you for generously dedicating your precious time to helping me make this the best cookbook there is.

TO MY BLOGGING FRIENDS—Rachel Currier, Gina Matsoukas, Megan Keno, Brandy O'Neill, Katrina Bahl, Erin Dooner, and many more. Thank you for constantly being there and for being an outlet to bounce around ideas. Your patience is appreciated! You all are a constant inspiration to me.

TO THE READERS OF *TABLEFORTWOBLOG.COM*—The blog and, quite frankly, the cookbook would not be here today without your constant support, feedback, and encouragement. I look forward to reading your e-mails and comments every day. Thank you for coming along on this journey with me, and I hope there are many more delicious years to come!

TO MY LAWYER, SARA HAWKINS—Thank you for constantly looking out for me and being there for guidance and advice. It has been most appreciated, and I look forward to future projects with you.

TO MY EDITOR, ANN TREISTMAN—Thank you for believing in me and for taking my idea and bringing it to life. Your guidance and expertise throughout this process has been greatly appreciated. It's been a rewarding and fulfilling experience. I hope to create more deliciousness with you!

Index